To Be Two

To Be Two

LUCE IRIGARAY

Translated by MONIQUE M. RHODES
and MARCO F. COCITO-MONOC

Routledge
New York

Published in 2001 by
Routledge
29 West 35th Street
New York, NY 10001

This edition published by arrangement with The Athlone Press
This English translation © The Athlone Press 2000
Originally published as *Essere Due* © Bollati Boringhieri 1994

Cataloging-in-Publication Data is available from the Library of Congress

ISBN 0–415–91807–3 (HB)
      0–415–91815–4 (PB)

Printed and bound in Great Britain

Contents

Translators' Acknowledgements

We should like to thank Luce Irigaray for her generous assistance while we prepared this translation. By supplying us with her unpublished seminar notes and by meeting with us on several occasions in Paris, she has deepened our appreciation of the importance and complexity of her overall project – something we hope has enhanced the translation which follows.

Additionally, we extend our thanks to Margaret Whitford for her continued support and advice, as well as for the excellent example of academic rigor which she has provided both within Irigaray studies and philosophy in general. We have profited in innumerable ways from the advice which Philippa Berry and Alison Martin have been kind enough to share with us on earlier drafts of select chapters, and from the steadfast friendship and good humor of Stephen Kee and Lee Barclay.

When I wrote *I Love to You*, I wanted to write it in Italian. After all, the book is dedicated to an Italian and Italian is the language of many of my ancestors. The publishers of the Italian edition of *I Love to You* (*Amo a Te*) and the translator of the book itself encouraged me in my decision to write *To be Two* in Italian. I thank my publishers just as I thank the two people who helped me by reading the Italian text, Caterina Resta and Adele Pesce.

1

Prologue

Just reborn from her

Earth,
you who house me but with whom I share,
you who are fecund with so many children, who do not
    resemble one another,
you who grow without respite, both in secret and in the light,
you who bear seed, flower and fruit,
you who never cease to repair life,
you who at every time of the year work for the becoming of
    the living,
allowing the lymph to rise or fall again, keeping it
from spilling out of you, except for the ripe fruit,
Earth,
you who are still lavish with sun when the frost comes,
Earth,
safeguard me, faithful one.

And when the spring returns, you laugh.
You rustle through the leaves and the flowers.
You quiver through the birds.
There is not the rapid growth of the first summer, but its joy.
The splendor of the year's mid-point has not yet burst forth,
    we are at the opening.
It is the time of the unfinished, of wonder.
Life walks on tiptoes.
Despite the songs of the birds, silence persists.
Is this not, perhaps, how what grows preserves its future?
Insuperable distances exist in the spring.
No space is yet fully occupied, but the spaces
are not empty: they are inhabited by an invisible growth.
Where it seems that nothing exists, there remains one presence,
    or a thousand.

There is the one, and the many; the one is the many.
But the separation has not yet taken place.
Earthly and celestial roots join together without usurping the
   limits of others.
Everyone remains in his or her birthplace, but the whole opens.

I am immersed in the spring: quiet, attentive. Gathered but
porous, I receive the environment's jubilation.[a] I do not accumu-
late, but become, growing in a new life. There is the felicity of the
beginning, of the breath still virginal.

Joy's laughter ripples. The iridescence of this morning leaves
union chaste: in us, between us. One hears clear and crystalline
notes, outbursts of children's laughter, songs of birds. One also
imagines angels whispering, souls quivering, while leaves and
flowers grow to become living bouquets. The flowers are light,
without pretense: ethereal, colored or only white. Smiles of the
spring, they bear witness to a muted hope. Life whispers. The
earth, like a great nest, houses us, nurses our rebirth.

The air, fluid density which leaves space for every growth.
Matter that, not yet divided in itself, permits sharing.

The air, stillness, gathering, harmony: in which I find myself
separated from but also linked with the whole, except for what
does not breathe.

The air, birth in familiarity with the vegetal. The world that
becomes a mother.

Why is it said that the universe is the work of the father? Does
it not, rather, resemble another mother?

Life's taste returns in her tenderness – sweet, warm, fragrant,
also caressing and rustling. She comforts us after every wound and,
playing around it, does not envelope us in any way but incites us to
feel, to leave pain in order to celebrate her, to praise her presence,
to contemplate her grace and to abandon those who forget her for
disincarnate enticements, for conflicts without either consequence
or motive if not the artifice of an energy separated from life.

The air which touches: invisible presence. Love's return everywhere. In this infinite being touched, the wound vanishes. The
first and last resource envelopes me: clouds or angels, down or soft
arms, smiles or words for children.

*

How do we humans share this cradle, this nest, these surround-ings? The plants live together without difficulty. And we? How do we share the air? Without the vegetal world, how do we live together? In fact, it substitutes for the mother. But, without either of these, how is the between-us possible? Can words protect the food which she lavishes? Do they travel the same air or another? Is this air suitable for life?

And if you are quiet, does this not mean that you lack words? And if you sing, is it not perhaps because there is more air in song: beyond the hither and yon of words?

Your silence exists, as does my self-gathering. But so does the almost absolute silence of the world's dawning. In such suspension, before every utterance on earth, there is a cloud, an almost immobile air. The plants already breathe, while we still ask ourselves how to speak, how to speak to each other, without taking breath away from them.

In such a garden resonates the song of the birds, those who celebrate the present moment, who assure the passage between here and there, between earth and sky.

Messengers, they announce if the site is livable. When the universe is not habitable, the birds, if only for a time, are mute. As soon as the danger draws away, they again communicate the celestial: nearby, they tell the distant.

If they speak, it is possible to stop and listen. When they remain silent, it is best to hurry. They indicate if a place is hospitable or not. As nature's angels, they come and go, visible and invisible, noisy or silent, according to whether there is tension or harmony.

They are not merely consumers of our gifts. Their vocalizations go beyond thanks for a few seeds. They mean much more.

At every hour their messages ring out, low or high-pitched, simply melodious or more immediately useful. They signal to those who sojourn on the earth the moment of the day, of the year, and also whether there is harmony or discord between the elements of the universe.

Between them is the moisture which protects silence and prepares a space without sound, save that of the rain and the birds. But nothing which comes from afar, carried by a dryer air.

Here, the nest is made of wet leaves; the touch, of wind and of water drops. With its roof closed, the grey itself produces the gathering. The breath searchingly sniffs out the beyond, and perhaps the crossing. But no color indicates the direction of the summit. The passage remains imperceptible to the gaze.

I enjoy listening to the earth. In listening, I rediscover bliss, the wonder of attentive perception, the happiness of sonorous flesh. It is not only a message which reaches me but a vibration which gladdens me. It plays at the limits of myself: still outside, but already within. Neither sound nor words, it is animated silence. The whiteness of life's rustling from which no word emerges, it is accompanied by a soft palpitation. It is seemingly nothing, if not the happiness of being with her, while remaining myself.

The sound of the living, the breath of the air, the joy of strength all resemble a word conveyed by her.

The meaning[b] is not perhaps completely clear, unless it is reduced to mirth. But, with her, I learn patience. I withdraw to listen, quiet. Leaving to be that which is, I await grace.

I sense the quiet in my body, the sweetness under my skin. Silence spreads, along with its presence: peaceful, alive. I intuit the arrival of another, nearby and yet distant, confused with the tenderness of repose. But in memory exists a mystery. Perhaps more than one lives in me with its veiled secret.

Will the familiar be reborn? The flower grows there, at times also the flame and the light. It remains in silence, like a gathered fidelity, the living matrix for a future. It seems a downy cradle where the newly born seeks refuge. It still lacks contours, definite limits, but it has already been conceived and is to be protected.

With love for her, the blue returns. Tenderness impregnates the air – like a presence. It seems that certain words are whispered. Perhaps the birds are confiding some secret to each other. The whole blooms in a still lofty atmosphere. Between earth and sky, a breath comes and goes, joining one to the other. Its scent is perhaps the most subtle incense.

In fact, to be in her, with her is enough. There remains work to complete: a house to build, a love to invent, a spirit to cultivate.

*

The air is sweet, carnal and silent. Its touch recalls the familiar. Happiness inhabits it. It is of a luminous blue, resolute but extremely tender. It seems a living being, a bridge, a relationship. A rainbow of spring.

Love for the star, desire for the light. And trust in her. Leaving myself to be in her, I renounce all apprehension and dedicate myself to welcoming. I hope for an appropriate gift from her, a present which is suited to me, a miracle in abandonment.

Returning to the sun. Delivering myself to her – life. Enveloped in her so thoroughly, the fear of offending her still lingers. Yet I remain in her arms, knowing that a day limits itself to a period of light, after which suddenly arrives the night.

Joy is in me. It lives in my body, rises like lymph. There it dwells, profound, grave, silent. It dissolves what divides me from myself: useless mental noise.

Now nothing separates us. Immersed in her, I share colors and light. I become her, becoming also myself. I respect her, respecting myself. I love her, loving myself. She is within me and outside of me. Certainly I cannot embrace her, but she is there. She surrounds me, radiates in me, illuminates me, comforts me, without a gift in exchange.

The quality of the air is almost perfect, the blue of the sky almost divine. At times, man sullies it, incapable of sustaining such splendor, such a tonality of happiness. Then the heart breaks and harmony is lost. Joy is dispersed in argument. Where angelic lightness once played, shadows impose themselves. They fall like rocks, weighing upon the soul, the air, the earth.

To repose in her, to contemplate with her, allowing myself to be contemplated. Beyond fixed desire, I am embracer-embraced. Porous, I am attentive without restraining. I return to myself to welcome without keeping, to love without loving. To love to her?

Her tenderness is there, immobile: in the air, the flowers, the blue of the sky. If the breath is placed in unison with them, all suffering vanishes. Love is in me. Leaping closures, it rises, breaking bonds, undoing paralyses. Without pain, it consoles, awakens, calms.

In this way, to discover the peace of the body, the harmony of the living. To leave the breath to its rhythm, like waves which come and go, in and out, out and in. The star accompanies this coming and going. The world resembles a single breath.

If the sun remains in me, more ardent, more like the morning, life is condensed. It resists dispersal, delighting to dwell in me; it lingers to love, seeking more to radiate than to diffuse itself. It gathers itself in order to spread itself, leaving secret what is offered. Whoever senses it can pause before it.

Her warmth seems a laugh which has blossomed and dazzled. In this tender effusion, we walk in happiness, in complicit silence, each of us giving ourselves to the other.

Who knows where we are going? Love bears the weight of time. The hours are clearer or darker, more burning or more fresh. The birds sing, turning to the day or to the night. I take refuge in her, waiting to return to the deepest part of myself, and waiting also for the arrival of the memory of another force.

To experience happiness, to rediscover the breath. To emerge from pain and choose bliss. Renouncing dominion, to love the earth until life resurges. I perceive her through all of my skin, immersed in her, leaving every thought, every screen behind. I am impregnated with her colors, with her smells. I open myself to the warmth of the air, to the light of the day, to the contemplation of what surrounds me.

The universe becomes carnal when I am with him,ᶜ close to him. As I contemplate his splendor, I do not forget the familiar. My intimate friend speaks to me, his presence made sweetness. I find rest in the universe, entrust myself to him. My eyes open themselves upon his glory, my heart is at peace. I seek the return within myself, the silence of his welcoming and, perhaps, that of your arrival.

The air is sweet. Its flowering is in harmony with presence: it is as tender as a caress. I raise love up to the word. I call upon fidelity to make a sign, or at the very least, a sound. I search for a voice inspired by you or which I want you to hear. I await the music of my heart, attentive all the while to yours.

I try to find a note which is neither too shrill nor too grave: the tonality of life inhabited by emotion, the song of an intention sustained by an ideal.

Might you, earth, not remain around me? Do I risk growing too much? Can I be alone and yet remain surrounded by you? Or will the other divide us? How do we remain two in you? Is it necessary to distance myself from you to walk towards him? Will you remain a support, a mother to whom nothing is given in exchange? For him, I need you, but how do I return to you? How do I thank you for your gifts? How do I make an alliance with him without sacrificing you? Is praise enough for you? Do you want nothing more? Nothing of us?

Is it not a form of exile to return again amongst humans? Is it not perhaps suicide to leave a fragrant dwelling, an ethereal intimacy, a diffuse presence and enter, instead, into the nothingness in which, all too often, the living move about?

Restless, chattering, forgetful, they wander about as if at home in a universe of death, entrusting their destiny to a few words. Unwittingly, they distance themselves from what lavishes life, counting and calculating without making sure their own steps or the values which guide them. They go. But where?

You, my stars, masters of the universe, are my guardians and my peace, the font of my duties and of my fortunes. Bound to you in some mysterious way, I try to be faithful without understanding. I welcome your commands. Attentive, I am sometimes amazed, sometimes terrified, even though, in a certain sense, I put more faith in you than in myself. When decisions frighten me, I search for a sign, not knowing if you are to guide me or if I am to guide you. I do not even know how to respect you in carrying out my own becoming.

A fresher breath springs up in me when I call you, when I affirm an ideal shared by our stars. Upon hearing their fate, I do not allow myself to be led astray by what is of no importance or remains without happiness.

Although the note may be high, it roots itself in the deepest profundity. It is not strained – it can be held with harmony.

He arrives

Your beauty – the beauty of the world. Your love – the beating of the universe, the loving rhythm of nature, time in harmony with the sun.

In you, I behold its radiance. In you, I savor its power, I bathe in its warmth. At times, the eternal joins with the instant. We are present to each other, but between us remains eternity, while we continue to grow. How do we unite these two times?

Will I not have placed the whole of the earth between us? How do I return to you? Can I enter into a relationship with you through her[d] – safeguarding her, cultivating her, purifying the air that she gives? Are we ultimately something other than she who becomes in us and outside of us? Is it not the perfection of the relationship with her that I behold in you? Is not such humility the spiritual reign itself? How do I call the going beyond? And how do I accomplish this without abandoning and destroying her?

Looking at the other, respecting the invisible in him, opens a black or blinding void in the universe. Beginning from this limit, inappropriable by my gaze, the world is recreated. I inhabit it, but the entirety of its truth is not mine; since it is not completely known to me, it remains sensible and alive. Suspending judgement thus permits the to be.[e] We can remain together if you do not become entirely perceptible to me, if a part of you stays in the night.

Already, beauty has created a distance: a veil over us. It seems a radiation of light softened by the flesh: a guardianship of you, of me, a repose for us and between us. It is not an incitement to go outside of the self, but is a gathering in the self. It is like a silent word, a living mystery, a dialogue beyond words. Union of the soul and body harmoniously linked, it is a gift of innocence, an illumination of shyness, a refolding of the body in its intention.

I regard you, then, as invisible, even if you are perceptible to my eyes: I see the diffusion of your interiority beyond your visible forms.

*

Do I not approach another kind of sensibility, neither active nor passive? I am sensible to you, leaving you to be you. I am sensible with you, each of us remaining ourselves. I sense you beyond the immediate. I am in your presence, certainly, but it cannot be reduced either to materiality or to abstraction. I brush against your spiritual substance. I behold your being without removing it from its invisibility: through my eyes, through my understanding.

But is my existence not protected by your irreducibility? Is the total other that you are not my guardian? Does such a distance not allow me to remain tangible? Does my faith in you not drive away every injury from me? Does it not draw a temple around me? Doubtless, such a temple is not made from a void but corresponds to a place which guarantees our difference.

The universe is our refuge, as is the certainty that we are two. Each remote from the other, we are kept alive by means of this insuperable gap. Nothing can ever fill it. But it is from such nothingness that a spring of the to be is derived for us. Is it not because I do not know you that I know that you are?[f]

Only love consents to a night in which I will never know you. Between those who love each other, there is a veil. In solitude, perhaps setting out with a lamp is necessary, but in love?

Does such a night correspond to blind faith or to respect for the one I will never know? Is it not this unknown which allows us to remain two?

The existence of a mystery safeguards each of us. In blindness, we remain distinct, one towards the other, perceiving each other through touch, however distant. Outside of all violence, we await the word addressed to us.

Leaving both of us to be – you and me, me and you –, never reducing the other to a mere meaning, to my meaning, we listen always and anew to each other so that the irreducible can remain.

For you, for us, between shadows and light. Always being in the light wounds. Modesty requires a bit of secrecy, a silence over what is known, a reserve: to respect you and leave obscurity between us.

Who I am for you and who I am for me is not the same,

and such a gap cannot be overcome. We are irreducible in us, between us, and yet so close. Without this difference, how do we give each other grace, how do we see each other, the one in the other?

I become because I recognize myself in you. But how do I express this becoming if not as growth and rebirth, such as happens in the spring?

What is left for me to say? How do I speak after the absolute has been confided forever? What can I express if not all that grows, if not an absolute more absolute than already exists?

Between you and me, what remains? The world itself? At this point, nothing else is possible if not the whole of the world. Between us, the world and all of creation. Restored to innocence, or invited to be so? Between us, all that I have learned to look upon, to live. Is this not the whole? At least the whole which existed before man appeared.

But between plant, animal, angel or god, we still lack the human. We still fall short of the human.

I perceive you as a man. By becoming a god, did you not choose your own downfall? I was not able to manifest my appearance: between the visible and invisible.

I beheld you as the one who allowed me concentration, already and not yet existent. Only the morning rouses attention, or rather growth. Only what becomes attracts, only what does not descend towards its setting.

To rediscover your presence, to return to tenderness, to inhabit the air of the us: diffuse ardor, dense lightness, with diverse tones, gestures differently mobile.

We move without effort, happy without thinking, hidden and transparent. We speak to each other in all languages: forgetting ours, knowing another. We are attentive to the meaning beyond the vehicle of language: never yours, never mine, inappropriable. We remain present to our senses, unclouded by any possession.

To return in me, to return to you. To distance the pain of usurpation, the insinuation of the foreign. To flee the appropriation of the inappropriable, the oblivion of the air, the appropriation of the to be[e] that is like breath between us.

Without anger, to drive away the intruder, to return him to himself, to push out whoever penetrates our horizon and thereby destroys it. And also: to remove the ambiguity from desire, the possession from love. To find myself freed from the heaviness which annihilates the space in me, the innocence in me, and the light between us.

With you, the world remains fluid. Words are ethereal. The sensible remains sweet and carnal: living, pulsating. It is light like the birds, the flowers, the angels. It is felicity. Fragile, too, in its incomplete incarnation.

How can the memory of this undiscovered sweetness, of this unknown and fragile felicity, be ensured? How can the warmth of the air within, this desirable but fleeting peace, be prolonged: all such evasive moments?

How will I protect joy? Where will I place it in myself? How will I inscribe it in the duration? How will I make it into a place for meditation, a font of spirituality? Gratitude and becoming: will joy then be a force? Your presence in me: fidelity.

Who or what will permit me to protect you? A retreat in the mountains? Solitude in the forest? The peace in myself? Perhaps you who will allow me to find rest in myself. Peaceful is the cloud where we hide, and from where the sun is born anew.

How do I remain in love – cultivating sun and grace? How do I flee injury, avoid drought, war which ignores alliance, science which takes no heed of the truth?

I have heard love and hate. One is sweet and silent, the other sharp and chattering. Many think that one does not go without the other, those who do not know how to communicate without words.

With whom do I cultivate the breath? Who will allow me to remain two: the one, the other, and the air between us? Life is taken from no one. Each one safeguards it for him or herself and for the other, existing in solitude thanks to nature, but still wanting to live with the other. Each one, therefore, trains the breath in order to be, to be and to become: divided between us, perhaps, but together at the same time. Distanced by our difference, but present to each other.

*

Are not the "you" and the "I" lost in loving, in merely loving? Is it not an act of sacrifice to love without the incarnation of love? Like a flame, a froth, self-consummation ascends to God.

How do I make the fire into a guardian, in the body, in beauty, in speech? How do I protect without restraining? In an alliance between the heart and an internal mirror? Is it a matter of thinking, tasting? Surely, it is a matter of feeling with and thanks to the other and, without consuming, contemplating his incarnation: the crossing between body and word.

The exchange takes place beyond instinct, renouncing the predatory gesture. But few understand it this way. Sharing the word does not mean believing: incarnation prevents blind faith, and requires that each person is present and speaking.

It is up to us to be faithful to this crossing: body and word. The universal becoming of the word distances itself from such fidelity, while speaking to each other accomplishes it, refusing every manner of sharing which is not also word. Neither body nor language simply, but incarnation between us: the word being flesh and the flesh word.

Thus I and you, she and he, speak to each other and each one forms a subjectivity denying access to the self and to the other prior to all speech. Between us are the world and the word and the universe and the word. One is, in part, common to us while the other remains unique to each of us. You remain a mystery to me through your body and through your word, and our alliance will always involve a mystery.

Certainly, genealogical difference makes us unknown to each other, but to a lesser degree than when the word becomes flesh and flesh becomes word. But such is the union between woman and man.

We need to love much to be capable of such a dialectic. One must love enough to generate and not wound: love the other as a whole, love him in his life without giving him one's own. Respect him as a font derived from his own alterity.

I cannot be the whole for him. I can neither exist nor be in his place. But I can perhaps give him a livable place, prepare a space around him, contain myself: approach myself while drawing away from myself. Return in me without scattering or dispersing myself.

*

Trust, it is true, restores the body to its integrity. It gathers itself in front of the other. This concentration of ourselves becomes possible thanks to our difference. In a relationship with those like me, I scatter and fragment myself. Between those that are alike, the infinite expands and multiplies, whereas an intensity exists in the relationship with the other.

When it is missing, this intensity is sought in genealogy. If I cannot attain my totality because you are irreducible to me, must I not seek shelter in a family, whether natural or spiritual?

Only your existence helps me to be born, to move out of my placenta. I discover the divine between us, conceived by us but not combined with us, existing between each of us. We give birth to it, adults at last. Arriving at another stage of our history, God reveals himself as the work of man and woman. It always awaits us, like a horizon between memory and alliance.

Is its name God? But the alliance with nature, what is its name?

Between us is something which will never be mine or yours. Would a vertical transcendence not rob us us of this third dimension beginning from which we approach each other as different others? Others in flesh and spirit. If the third dimension is found in the beyond, we become images-of, reduced to two dimensions, with a bit more subjectivity and with a bit more or a bit less of the object: phallus or baby.

If transcendence is between us, recognizing you as other perhaps implies giving you up to your solitude, and also to your volume, to you, an incarnate subject: in you, outside of you, other than me, with air and perspective between us. Thus we are body and soul for each other.

I want to live in harmony with you and still remain other. I want to draw nearer to you while protecting myself for you. It pleases me to protect for you the freshness of unknown flesh and the discovery which brings awakening.

To foster growth in difference: tender happiness. This grace flickers across my lips, my heart, my thoughts. I love you upon the threshold of this permanent alterity, offered to my attentive senses and spirit. I wish that the flowers themselves could help me in such fidelity.

Will you, sky, be the one to whom I turn to address my song?

Will I send it towards your deep blue flesh? Or will I sing to the one who lives far away?

How can I speak to you: find the words, discover the tone, touch you without losing myself? To touch you and thus exist beginning from the two. The listening which permits you to be makes it possible for you to hear me. Between us is created a field of life's vibrations intersected with those of the universe. United to the earth and to the sky, we are supported by our horizontality, sustained by it, by us. This force protects our equilibrium: despite gravity, we are lifted slightly above the ground, while remaining faithfully on the earth.

To sense you, to preserve a place for you and to speak to you beginning from this memory. To find tone, rhythm, meaning. To cultivate the breath until the words can rise up in me and pass the threshold of myself.

May I find them and carry them up to you! May they be born and dwell in me, in you. Not as truth but as faithfulness to us.

To perceive what the other is, while not knowing it. Not to use such knowledge but to make my gaze helpful to him: an aid, a resource. And to accept that he will be the one who discovers of innocence lives there, if it is capable of contemplating without violence or capture: to insist on transcendence here and now, with us and between us.

From my listening, perhaps silence will be born. Being attentive to you will silence the din, will give birth to a world where we can remain, a place where we can live and collect ourselves, a space where we can rest and savor happiness.

A new wonder will be born, an innocent and native gaze, an extraordinary day.

To be silent to allow you to speak, to give birth to you. And to us, as well.

To listen to the other's love. To contemplate this gift of restrained vibration. Instead of scattering joy about, to transform it into praise, into hymns, into felicity: an alchemy of energy, a return to myself. The result is not something in excess, but an other. The breath is conserved so that we may speak in a new way: speak love not only with gestures of the body but also with gestures of the word.

Because I love you absolutely, I, myself, am no longer absolute. Recognizing you gives me measure. Because you are, you impose limits upon me. I am whole, perhaps, but not the whole. And if I receive myself from you, I receive myself as me. We are no longer one. Contemplating each other, we do not lose either the night or the light. Each can leave to the other his or her own life: sun, moon, stars. Being faithful to you requires being faithful to me. Does existing not mean offering you an opportunity to become yourself?

Where we are constrained to fusion, to discover a gap. Where language unites us fictitiously, to return to our difference. Where others assimilate us to themselves, to safeguard our autonomy. Where some desire to consume us, to preserve a distance.

To drive away what intervenes between us. To protect the world and maintain the negative. To push to the outside of our relationship everything which disturbs, quantifies and compares. To repel whoever envies, mimes and wishes to appropriate. To distance whoever pretends to be or to rob me of who I am, you of who you are, us of who we are. To collect ourselves until we can escape all of these dangers.

To save myself not in view of an object but for an other. Not to bind myself to nothingness but to leave within me a ready place. Is it not perhaps the welcoming of the other which safe-guards this clearing? Is it not this which permits respect and generation, which encourages becoming, birth and rebirth? Desired opening. Gathering within a chaste intention.

But in which part of myself do I preserve you? In which breath? How do I remain without suffocating? How do I make earth out of air, and protect the cloud in me? Where are you prior to your incarnation? Where I dwell with you?

In sharing with others, there is a calm restraint, a soul: a resource for me, a memory of you.

I have not consumed you. The matter of your passage and of your coming lives in me. Joy remains in me, maintaining the bridge between past and future.

*

How do I return to myself and descend into my heart without you? Is it possible to arrive there alone? Does solitude not extend itself from my feet to my head and beyond? To be two would allow us to remain in ourselves, would permit gathering, and the type of safeguarding which does not restrain, the kind of presence which remains free of bonds: neither mine nor yours but each living and breathing with the other. It would refrain from possessing you in order to allow you to be – to be in me, as well.

To lean on you, not just on your body, but to be carried by your spirit: inspired by you, inhabited by you, resplendent with your strength. Trusting in such becoming, neither greedy nor blameworthy, I consent with[g] songs of praise.

If transcendence exists between us, if we are visible and invisible to each other, the gap is enough to sustain our attraction. Why should an object between us be necessary? To be irreducible to one another can assure the two and the between, the us and the between-us. And from where would the need for appropriation arise, if each allows the other to return to his or her to be?

Consuming does not produce one's existence. Instead, difference can protect this existence: I am if you are, to be together with you allows me to become. The two, this two, is the bit more which is indispensable if I am to be. Closing myself up in consumption, in possession, in production, does not make me one. What makes me one, and perhaps even unique, is the fact that you are and I am not you.

2

The wedding between the body and language

My experience as a woman demonstrates, as does my analysis of the language of women and men,[1] that women almost always privilege the relationship between subjects, the relationship with the other gender, the relationship between two.

Certainly, there are other features characteristic of the feminine world, but it is interesting to compare the three just mentioned with three particular aspects of masculine being and speaking.

With men, one finds both a material and spiritual relationship between subject and object in place of the intersubjective relationship – however incomplete – desired by women. There is another difference: the relationship with the object, with the other, with the world is realized through an instrument which can be the hand, sex, and even a tool added to the body, language, or a third mediator. Finally, instead of the feminine universe's relationship between two, man prefers a relationship between the one and the many, between the I-masculine subject and others: people, society, understood as *them* and not as *you*.

These differences between the being and speaking of woman and man can help us to interpret the way in which male philosophers – such as Jean-Paul Sartre, Maurice Merleau-Ponty and Emmanuel Lévinas – have conceived carnal love, and can make apparent the feminine character of my words on loving relations, particularly on the caress.

For Jean-Paul Sartre, the body of the other is a "facticity",[2] a fact, a present objective reality, which is beside me. As such, the other is that which I can see and touch. But the other is more than facticity, the other is consciousness: of-itself, for-itself, consciousness of the world, even.

Given that consciousness is transcendent with respect to the body – as Sartre and the majority of Western philosophers think – the other exists beyond what is perceived as a fact.

If this is the case, how do I desire the other and enter into a carnal relationship with him? In *Being and Nothingness*, Jean-Paul Sartre maintains that the only possible way is to enchant him. It is a matter of making his consciousness descend into his body, of paralyzing his liberty in the factuality of a body. The consciousness of the other must be coagulated in his body – "as one says of a coagulated cream or mayonnaise" – in such a way that the for-itself of the other can surface in his skin, his consciousness can extend itself throughout the entire surface of his body, so that, touching this body, "I . . . finally touch the other's[a] free subjectivity."[3]

Thus, I can "possess" the other and, according to Sartre, the fulfillment of desire does not exist without such possession: the fact that the other is already a body possessed of a consciousness determines the desire to possess it. This male philosopher represents the impossible ideal of desire in the following way: the transcendence of the other is to be possessed as pure transcendence inaccessible to sensible experience, but nevertheless as body.

After this hunt for the freedom of the other, the lovers' awakenings are not so happy, paralyzed and weakened as they are in the "facticity" of their bodies.

Desire that wants only the same cannot escape conflict in order to appropriate the other's transcendence.

Emphasizing the difference between man and woman leads to a new consideration of their carnal approach and union.

If both become by linking themselves to a vertical transcendence appropriate to their gender, there is another transcendence between them. For those who are faithful to their own gender, this horizontal transcendence cannot be overcome. The conflict which arises from the appropriation of the freedom of the other no longer makes sense between those who love each other: desire grows from an irreducible alterity.

The other is and remains transcendent to me through a body, through intentions and words foreign to me: "you who are not and will never be me or mine" are transcendent to me in body and in words, in so far as you are an incarnation that cannot be appropriated by me, lest I should suffer the alienation of my freedom. The will to possess you corresponds to a solitary and solipsistic dream which forgets that your consciousness and mine do not obey the same necessities.

Rather than grasping you – with my hand, with my gaze, with my intellect – I must stop before the inappropriable, leaving the transcendence between us to be. "You who are not and will never be me or mine" are and remain *you*, since I cannot grasp you, understand you, possess you. You escape every ensnarement, every submission to me, if I respect you not so much because you are transcendent to your body, but because you are transcendent to me.

Far from wanting to possess you in linking myself to you, I preserve a "to", a safeguard of the in-direction between us – *I Love to You*, and not: I love you. This "to" safeguards a place of transcendence between us, a place of respect which is both obligated and desired, a place of possible alliance. You do not, then, find yourself reduced to a factual thing or to an object of my love, and not even to an ensemble of qualities, which make you into a whole perceivable by me. Instead, I stop in front of you as in front of an other irreducible to me: in body and in intellect, in exteriority and in interiority.

It is not necessary to bestow upon the other a capital letter, an excessively quantitative valuation, in order to make this other's transcendence appear. Such a valuation places transcendence beyond you, where it annuls and repudiates you as *you*, you-other for I-me. This capitalization of the Other paralyzes us by means of a fictitious freedom, by means of an absence from ourselves, extasies from our incarnation. In fact, the consciousness represented by this "O" remains exterior to a language which is made flesh in you, in me, in us. Before being law or truth exterior to us, "consciousness outside of us", as Sartre writes, language should make our body and our history into a single subjectivity, possibly in relationship with the subjectivity of the other. Does language not exceed its own power, truth, ethicality, as long as it is not the way for being I in me and I with you?

Certainly, I will never understand you, I will never grasp who you are: you will always remain outside of me. But this not being *I*, not being *me*, or *mine*, makes speech possible and necessary between us.

No manner of speaking about desire is valid without this muted question: "Who are you who will never be me or mine, you who will always remain transcendent to me, even if I touch you, since the word is made flesh in you in one way, and in me in another?"

In their desire for the other, male philosophers generally evoke sight and touch. Thus, like their hand, their gaze grasps, denudes and captures. The transcendence of the other, however, requires that the invisible in him be respected, including when he is perceived with the senses. Beyond the color of his eyes, the tone of his voice, the quality of his skin, things that are sensible to me, for me, there exists in the other a subjectivity which I cannot see, either with my senses or with my intellect. Male thinkers dodge this irreducible invisible, choosing not to appeal to language as a path towards sharing the mystery of the other.

In a passage from *The Phenomenology of Perception* dealing with the "sexuate body", Maurice Merleau-Ponty discusses the relationship between modesty and immodesty in a way which recalls Jean-Paul Sartre's treatment of enchantment, possession, and the amorous ambiguity that is born from belonging both to a body and to a consciousness.

There is no doubt at all that we must recognize in modesty, desire and love in general a metaphysical significance, which means that they are incomprehensible if man is treated as a machine governed by natural laws, or even as a "bundle" of instincts, and that they are relevant to man as a consciousness and as a freedom. Usually man does not show his body, and, when he does, it is either nervously or with an intention to fascinate. He has the impression that the alien gaze which runs over his body is stealing it from him, or else, on the other hand, that the display of his body will deliver the other person up to him, defenceless, and that in this case the other will be reduced to servitude. Shame and immodesty, then, take their place in a dialectic of the self and the other which is that of master and slave: in so far as I have a body, I may be reduced to the status of an object beneath the gaze of another person, and no longer count as a person for him, or else I may become his master and, in my turn, look at *him*. But this mastery is self-defeating, since, precisely when my value is recognized through the other's desire, he is no longer the person by whom I wished to be recognized, but a being fascinated, deprived of his freedom, and who therefore no longer counts in my eyes. Saying that I have a body is thus a way of saying that I can be seen as an object and that I try to be seen as a subject, that another can be my master or my slave, so that shame and shamelessness express the dialectic of the plurality of consciousness, and have a metaphysical significance. The same might be said of sexual desire: if it cannot accept the presence of a third party as witness, if it feels that too natural an attitude or over-casual remarks, on the part of the desired person, are signs of hostility, this is because it seeks to fascinate, and because the observing third person or the party desired, if he is too free in manner escapes this fascination. What we try to possess, then, is not just a body, but a body brought to life by consciousness (...) The importance we attach to the body and the contradictions of love are, therefore, related to a more general drama which arises from the metaphysical structure of my body, which is both an object for others and a subject for myself.[4]

The desired possession, therefore, is not just the possession of a body, but of a body animated by consciousness, a suggestion which also has much in common with that made by Jean-Paul Sartre.

My first critique of this pessimistic phenomenology would be that, in so far as I belong to a gender, my body already represents an objectivity for me. Therefore, I am not a simple subjectivity which seeks an object in the other. Belonging to a gender allows me to realize, in me, for me – and equally towards the other – a dialectic between subjectivity and objectivity which escapes the dichotomy between subject and object.

But the subject-object dichotomy also depends upon the manner in which sexuality itself is conceived. Maurice Merleau-Ponty considers sexuality as "ambiguity" and "indeterminacy", which are related not only to the body but to life in general. As a result, sexuality does not favor the emergence of intersubjectivity but, instead, maintains a duplicity in subjectivity itself in such a way that all of its actions, its sentiments, its sensations are ambiguous, murky, and incapable of being turned towards an other as such.

Similarly sexuality, without being the object of any intended act of consciousness, can underlie and guide specified forms of my experience. Taken in this way, as an ambiguous atmosphere, sexuality is co-extensive with life. In other words, ambiguity is of the essence of human existence, and everything we live or think has always several meanings (...) Thus there is in human existence a principle of indeterminacy, and this indeterminacy is not only for us, it does not stem from some imperfection of our knowledge, and we must not imagine that any God could sound our hearts and minds and determine what we owe to nature and what to freedom. Existence is indeterminate in itself, by reason of its fundamental structure (...) There is no explanation of sexuality which reduces it to anything other than itself, for it is already something other than itself, and indeed if we like, our whole being. Sexuality, it is said, is dramatic *because* we commit our whole personal life to it. But just why do we do this? Why is our body, for us, the mirror of our being, unless because it is a *natural self*, a current of given existence, with the result that we never know whether the forces which bear us on are its or ours- or with the result rather that they are never entirely either its or ours. There is no outstripping of sexuality any more than there is any sexuality enclosed within itself. No one is saved and no one is totally lost.[5]

In such a phenomenology, it seems that Maurice Merleau-Ponty is forgetting the function of sexuality as a relationship-to and that he is overlooking the role of perception as a means of acceding to the other as other. Perception represents a possible path for sensing the other, respecting him as subject, and it also allows me to remain a subject while perceiving the other. Perception can establish a link between the reception of a fact exterior to me and an intention towards the world, towards the other.

But our tradition is not dedicated to the cultivation[b] of sensible perception. We are accustomed to living thought as a night of the senses, as a transmission of language and its truth, without putting either of these to the test of everyday perception. Already in Plato's work, the handmaidens laugh at the philosophers who fall into wells because they fail to look at what is around them and are oblivious to the holes in their way. Another example: all of the great spiritual masters – apart, perhaps, from those who live in nature? – have testified to the necessity of having a woman close to them, better still if she is a virgin or spiritual mother, to act as a living memory of the common sense of everyday life. But, more generally, it seems that a man weds to have a woman in his home who will remind him of his immediate context and of sensible perception.

As a contrast to our tradition which does not heed the cultivation of perception, it is interesting to read several Far Eastern texts. I am thinking especially of the *Upanishad* of yoga, of several *sutras* of Patañjali, of Buddha's gaze upon the flower (see *I Love to You*). Buddha's contemplation of the flower suggests that we learn to perceive the world around us, that we learn to perceive each other between us: as life, as freedom, as difference.

Such a cultivation of perception would modify our loving relationships, whether intimate or communal. In fact, there is no rupture between intersubjectivity in the strict sense and the intersubjectivity of a collectivity, and the desired changes in the relations between man and woman, men and women, form part of a transformation which is helpful to all of our social relationships.

Merleau-Ponty's text shows that we lack a culture of perception and, because of this flaw, we fall back into the realm of simple feeling.

But sensation corresponds to a more passively lived experience and leads to a partitioning of intersubjectivity between two poles: a pole of the subject and a pole of the object. Sensation, sensations are divided according to a dichotomous logic: pleasure/pain, hot/cold and also active/ passive, masculine/feminine, along with other dichotomies which exile the body from its organization in a whole and from its incarnation via language, a language which remains, for this reason, distinguished by listening and fecundity.

This elementary economy of sensation is too abstract for the life of the flesh, for its harmony, for intersubjectivity, and causes sensibility to decline into simple "experience". The fact that loving relations are, for the most part, considered a sort of decadence, seems to come from a tradition of the sensible which has no respect for intersubjectivity or the exchange of words between those who love each other. This tradition reduces the feminine to a passive object which must experience sensation, while man must distance himself from woman in order to protect his relationship both with the realm of the intelligible and with his God.

As far as sensibility is concerned, we lack a culture which is subjective and intersubjective. Such a culture would require being faithful to the reciprocity in touching-being touched, itself a matter of perceiving or of speaking.

Also in communal relationships, the objective of words, their linguistic and phonetic economy, as well as their syntactic production, should be made to preserve a reciprocal touching in the act of communication. If a discourse or a collective organization prevent us from remaining in or returning to intersubjectivity, it is worth considering their potential as a totalitarian and deadly power.

Before suggesting the elements of a new philosophy of the caress, I will cite some passages from Lévinas taken from the chapter, "Phenomenology of Eros", in *Totality and Infinity*. My aim is to unveil certain tendencies in this philosopher's thought having to do with intersubjectivity and to highlight the differences between his philosophy and the intention of a woman in love. It is a way of responding to Lévinas' desire for a feminine discourse on virginity and on a possible carnal future for woman, for those who love each other.

 The caress consists in seizing upon nothing, in soliciting what ceaselessly escapes its form toward a future never future enough, in soliciting what slips away as though it *were not yet*. It [and I wish to add: this is man's caress] *searches*, it forages. It is not an intentionality of disclosure but of search (...) In a certain sense it *expresses* love, but suffers from an inability to tell it. It is hungry for this very expression, in an unremitting increase of hunger (...) The desire that animates it is reborn in its satisfaction, fed somehow by what *is not yet* , bringing us back to the virginity, forever inviolate, of the feminine (...) Beyond the consent or the resistance of a freedom the caress seeks *what is not yet*, a "less than nothing", closed and dormant beyond the *future*, consequently dormant quite otherwise than the *possible*, which would be open to anticipation. [And since this goes beyond the possible, there is always profanation in the caress]. The profanation which insinuates itself in caressing responds adequately to the originality of this dimension of absence (...) In the caress, a relation yet, in one aspect, sensible, the body already denudes itself of its very form, offering itself as erotic nudity. In the carnal given to tenderness, the body quits the status of existent [it is no longer the flower which Buddha contemplates]. The Beloved, at once graspable but intact in her nudity, beyond object and face and thus beyond the existent,

abides in virginity. The feminine essentially violable and inviolable, the "Eternal Feminine," is the virgin or an incessant
recommencement of virginity, the untouchable in the very
contact of voluptuosity, future in the present (...) The virgin
remains ungraspable, dying without murder, swooning, with-
drawing into her future, beyond every possible promise to
anticipation. Alongside of the night as anonymous rustling of
the *there is* extends the night of the erotic, behind the night of
insomnia the night of the hidden, the clandestine, the mysterious, land of the virgin, simultaneously uncovered by *Eros* and
refusing *Eros* – another way of saying: profanation. The caress
aims at neither a person nor a thing. It loses itself in a being
that dissipates as though into an impersonal dream without will
and even without resistance, a passivity, an already animal or
infantile anonymity, already entirely at death. The will of the
tender [and that through which Lévinas essentially fixes the
feminine] is produced in its evanescence as though rooted in an
animality ignorant of its death, immersed in the false security
of the elemental, in the infantile not knowing what is happening
to it.[6]

Beyond the fact that Lévinas thinks beginning only with himself, as man, and not in two or the reciprocity therein, there are
many differences between his phenomenology of the caress and
the one which I am attempting to think. Certainly, the differences
are not limited to the gesture of caressing but also testify to a
conception of carnal love which bears no resemblance to the eros
of Lévinas.
    The caress is an awakening to you, to me, to us.
    The caress is a reawakening to the life of my body: to its skin,
senses, muscles, nerves, and organs, most of the time inhibited,
subjugated, dormant or enslaved to everyday activity, to the
universe of needs, to the world of labor, to the imperatives or
restrictions necessary for communal living.
    The caress is an awakening to intersubjectivity, to a touching
between us which is neither passive nor active; it is an awakening
of gestures, of perceptions which are at the same time acts,
intentions, emotions. This does not mean that they are ambiguous,
but rather, that they are attentive to the person who touches and
the one who is touched, to the two subjects who touch each other.

The caress is an awakening to a life different from the arduous everyday. It is a call to a return to you, to me, to us: as living bodies, as two who are different and co-creators. It is a common act and work, irreducible to those acts and works dedicated either to individual or collective needs.

The caress is a gesture-word which goes beyond the horizon or the distance of intimacy with the self. This is true for the one who is caressed and touched, for the one who is approached within the sphere of his or her incarnation, but it is also true for the one who caresses, for the one who touches and accepts distancing the self from the self through this gesture.

Thus, the gesture of the one who caresses has nothing to do with ensnarement, possession or submission of the freedom of the other who fascinates me in his body. Instead, it becomes an offering of consciousness, a gift of intention and of word addressed to the concrete presence of the other, to his natural and historical particularities. To caress is to be aware of the qualities veiled in communal life, qualities that civil laws and practices should guarantee to all, removed from the violence of an everyday life which has no concern for intersubjectivity, removed from the violence of utilitarian practice – whether it involves commerce in the strict sense or the commerce of sexual desire – removed from a gaze or a practice not concerned with respecting the other.

The caress is a gesture-word which penetrates into the realm of intimacy with the self in a privileged space-time. It is a gesture which goes beyond the civil cloak or border of a proper identity, which exceeds the right to exist as a subject with one's own gender: a male or a female subject.

In order to go beyond a limit, there must be a boundary. To touch one another in intersubjectivity, it is necessary that two subjects agree to the relationship and that the possibility to consent exists. Each must have the opportunity to be a concrete, corporeal and sexuate subject, rather than an abstract, neutral, fabricated, and fictitious one.

It is important that each has been able to assent freely before the other approaches and goes beyond the sphere of subjective integrity, an integrity which should be protected by a right.

A *yes* from both should precede every caress.

A *yes* which gives permission to go beyond the limits of communal life towards your concrete presence.

A *yes* which is proof of my consent to your approach to my body, to my sensibility and to my most intimate language, all of which are foreign to the coexistence between citizens.

The caress is the spell directed at you in a way which is irreducible to the common, to the general, to the relative neutralization required by collective life. It is the awakening of you to yourself, and also to me. It is the call to be us, between us.

The caress is also praise. It is an homage of the evening, of the feast, of the spring to what I have perceived, sensed and experienced of you during the day, the week, the winter, during daily life clothed in the grey of ordinary demands, of urban transit, of the submission of sensible rhythms to the instruments of labor and to the rules of citizenship.

The caress is an invitation to rest, to relax, to perceive, to think and to be in a different way: one which is more quiet, more contemplative, less utilitarian.

The caress is a gift of safety, a call to return to yourself through the rediscovery of your virginity, here and now, thanks to me and us: your virginity understood not as a simply physical or phantasmic thing which is lost or preserved, violable or inviolable, and thus always beyond, never present but still and yet future (to speak as Lévinas does). I think of virginity, instead, as your repose with yourself, in yourself, you as irreducible to me, irreducible to what is common in community. Rather than violating or penetrating the mystery of the other, rather than reducing his or her consciousness or freedom to passivity, objectuality, animality or infancy, the caress makes a gesture which gives the other to himself, to herself, thanks to an attentive witness, thanks to a guardian of incarnate subjectivity.

The caress leads each person back to the *I* and to the *you*. I give you to yourself because you are a *you* for me. You remain you thanks to the *you* which you are for me, which you are "to" me – to recall the "to" of *I Love to You*, which has nothing to do with possession. Your body does not resemble an object for me, as subject, and the same is true for my body. For me, an incarnate subject, you are an incarnate subject. We are two woven of bodies and words, beings and to-bes,ᶜ and not merely beings under the spell of a master who vanish in imagined virginity.

An invitation to peacefulness instead of to passivity, the caress unfolds as an intersubjective act, as a communication between two, a call to an in-stasy in us and between us, and not to an ecstasy outside of us.

I would not say that desire makes the body ambiguous or equivocal, but rather that it renders it I-me together with I-you. A double intention animates me: I want to return to myself, in myself, and I want to be with you.

For this reason, the sexuate body and the sexual relationship are not bewitching or possession, submersion or nausea (as Sartre writes in *Being and Nothingness*), they are not ambiguity (according to the language of Merleau-Ponty in *Phenomenology of Perception*, "The Body in its Sexual Being"), and the feminine body, or the feminine, is not equivocation (as Lévinas suggests in *Totality and Infinity*). Enchantment, possession, ambiguity and equivocation alike signify a two which expresses both the existence and absence of two subjects as well as of intersubjectivity.

In my desire for you, in the love that I share with you, my body is animated by the desire to be with you or to you, with me or to me, and it also longs for the existence of a between-us. It wishes to love and to be loved, to leave itself and to re-enter itself. Wanting to go towards you and still attempt the return in myself, I seek an alliance between who you are and who I am, in myself and in yourself. I seek a complex marriage between my interiority and that of a *you* which cannot be replaced by me, which is always outside of me, but thanks to which my interiority exists.

If I go astray, it is not so much because of an ambiguity or an equivocation between the body's materiality and a more or less aroused consciousness; if I lose the way, it does not happen because of a confusion between subjectivity and objectivity or "facticity," and not even because there is a wavering of identity between you and me, between who you are and who I am, but rather because I wonder how to sustain a relationship between us, between two facts of body and language, between two intentions constituting an incarnate relationship which is realized by flesh and words.

In this double desire, "you" and "I" always remain active and passive, perceiving and experiencing, awake and welcoming. In us, sensible nature and the spirit become in-stance by remaining within their own singularity and grow through the risk of an exchange with what is irreducible to oneself.

3

Daughter and woman

In his philosophy, Sartre tries to place the corporeal relationship with the other in a horizontal dimension. While he does not reduce this relation to genealogy, he does tend to neglect each subject's history and its impact upon the present encounter with the other, with others.

In fact, the first relationship with the other is a bodily one, and it is not possible to speak of a horizontal relationship with the other without taking this into consideration. The first other which I encounter is the body of the mother, and this encounter differs depending upon whether I am a girl or a boy. This difference in the first relation with the other's body can enter into the constitution of woman's or man's identity. In so much as they are different, in body and in history, each can reassume the first relationship with the mother in their interiority so that they can escape its infinite repetition, one which alienates their present relationship.

For Sartre, the relationship with the other leads to an escape forward towards an impossible future: I must flee in the face of the other while giving myself the in-itself of the for-itself, making myself into my own substance, into a body born of my consciousness.

The for-itself is constituted in the same escape. It is surrounded by the in-itself, and it leaves such a prison only because it is nothing. The for-itself of Sartre is the foundation of this negativity and of this relationship. It corresponds to the relationship itself: between me and myself, the self and the self, the in-itself and the in-itself, is the abstract relationship, born only of a negativity.

The becoming which I propose is different. In so far as I belong to a gender, my body – the Ego-in-itself, as Sartre would say – already involves a for-itself. It is not simple factuality or "facticity", but is already consciousness. This cannot be reduced to a flight forward towards an in-itself that I would confer upon myself through and through. It must be a return towards me, in me, which cultivates that being which I am: a sexuate body, a body potentially animated by a consciousness which is my own.

Moreover, my body is inhabited by a consciousness which begins with its first relationship with the parental other, with the mother in particular. Such a relation is not neutral: it is sexuate. To say, for example, that the daughter must leave the mother in order to turn towards the father is to abolish her consciousness in so far as it is concrete, corporeal. From this moment, the subject enters into a determination of consciousness foreign to an incarnate relationship, and to the other. Already a conscious being, this subject thinks as a being outside of itself in an abstract transcendence both of the body and of its concrete relationship with the other, a consciousness which is at the same time external to itself and solipsistic.

When Sartre describes the corporeal relation between subjects, he situates it in a conception of consciousness which negates the first carnal and sexuate relationship with the other. The relationship is "concrete", according to Sartre, when it is corporeal. But the corporeal is already split between a consciousness-gaze and a body-facticity, both of which are disincarnate. There is no longer a bridge between the body and the consciousness. Where Sartre speaks of the pre-given, he describes it as a thing without intention. In fact, intention exists both on the part of the mother towards the girl or boy, and on the part of the child towards the mother. Thus, the affectionate gaze of the mother towards the body of her son and of her daughter, as well as their attention towards the mother, is forgotten in Sartre's thought.

This annulment of my attention towards the parental other, in particular towards the mother, and of her intention towards me, makes this Sartrian consciousness – and perhaps the consciousness of the whole of Western philosophy? – into a consciousness which is neither ethical nor true. It represents, perhaps, a means of participating in the life and culture of a community, in a certain epoch of history, but it is not the way for consciousness to be in-itself-for-itself here and now with an other. Since the first relationship between two consciousnesses has been erased, each one has been transformed into a zombie, into a neutral individual, into an abstract creature. The concrete encounter with the other, entering into carnal presence together with him, has become impossible. We are no longer two, but subjugated, both of us, to an abstract order which divides us into one+one+ ... parts of a community. We are, in a certain sense, shareholders of an abstract conscious- ness. Even supposing that everyone possesses the same number of shares of this capital of consciousness, the fact remains that the subject is already an automaton and an imperialist despot: "Any sort of other is too much for him", as Sartre writes. He wants to be alone in the world, and a relationship with the other corre- sponds to "hell".

As Sartre imagines it, the relation with the body of the other entails a double annulment of subjectivity, such as that of the feminine: both as daughter of a mother, and as a woman destined to the other gender, with a respect for the differences between them.

In my present body I am already intention towards the other, intention between myself and the other, beginning in genealogy. Although conceived outside of my parents' desire, although raised by them with little love and skill, I am still written in their intentions and animated by my own, whether conscious or uncon- scious, autonomous or interwoven with theirs. My body is never simple factuality or "facticity", unless it is a denial, an annulment of these intersubjective relationships which, from infancy, have marked it.

The spiritual ideal suggested by our tradition often erases intersubjective relations. In this tradition, our consciousness should overcome our corporeal and affective infancy by overturning it and substituting an abstract and solipsistic universe for it. The girl and boy, once in a world of relationships, should now become individuals contiguous to one another and yet separated. If the relationship with the other resembles hell, the cause could be precisely this abstract consciousness which dominates, alienates and erases the child in us. We are no longer animated by love, by language, by intentions; each of us is a nothing of existence, an existence in which the life of the pre-given has become a flight towards an impossible future. While Sartre takes the flight to be his task, Lévinas assigns it to the virginity of the feminine.

Desired, loved – however badly ... – by those who have produced us, we cannot annul this first part of our history without damaging our relationship with the other. Moreover, if we do not make ourselves responsible for this first relation, we regress into various types of infantile matrices and associations: a blind belonging either to private or public families, a propensity for primary institutions, for types of knowledge which are definite in a way which is dogmatic and closed, etc ... We must integrate into our in-itself-for-itself the given of an original relationship with our mother, with our parents, in which, at one time, we received life rather than death from the other.

Belonging to a gender must intervene in the in-itself-for-itself, in our body-consciousness. In so far as I am a sexuate being, I represent a meaning for the other and I am, in a way, destined to him. An intention is pre-given in my body, a for-itself is inscribed in it: relationships with my gender and with the other gender are inscribed as different ones. My body is not, therefore, a simple "facticity"; it is a relationship-with: with me, with my gender, with the other gender ... The body itself is intentionality: vertical in genealogy, horizontal in the relation between the genders.

Denying this intentionality means submitting myself to a consciousness abstracted from my incarnation, a consciousness which behaves like a terrifying lord, a sadistic master.

Upon entering into a relationship with the other, in particular with the other of sexual difference, my body is no longer a factuality or "facticity". By reducing itself to this statute, it annuls a consciousness already in it.

Furthermore, because it is sexuate, my body is, to a certain degree, destined to the other. Belonging to a gender represents a destination to the other more than it represents a biological destiny. To be born woman, before signifying to be humanity's reproducer, means to incarnate woman's to be with the other-man, together with man's to be.

Humanity reaches fulfillment between the two genders. The birth of a girl or a boy goes hand in hand with a destination involving the accomplishment of her or his own gender, and a destination involving the fulfillment of humanity together with the other gender.

Sexual difference is part of human identity in so far as it is a privileged dimension of the human being and of his or her fulfillment. To conceive the subject as one, as singular, as one and many, as one and as an ensemble of ones, is tantamount to misunderstanding an essential property of human existence and essence.

But this property cannot be expressed in the same categories which constitute or describe a singular subject. This property: being sexuate, implies a negative, a not being the other, a not being the whole, and a particular way of being: tied to the body and in relationship with the other, including therein the return to the self.

Far from fleeing towards an impossible future (as Sartre holds to be necessary in the relationship between the for-itself and the in-itself, or as Lévinas maintains, in a slightly different way, in the relationship of the feminine with virginity), the gesture here becomes a fulfillment of the self as body, as for-the-other, as a destination inscribed in the properties of my body. This other can be of my gender or of another, but it is above all to the other gender as other that I am destined.

It is not a matter of simple complementarity or supplementarity between the genders. We are not complementary or supplementary to each other. Rather, the question is how to think an identity which is different from the one we know, an identity in which the relationship with the other is inscribed in the pre-given of my body.

Certainly, I can decide to become woman while suspending the empirical relationship with the other gender – on account of historical impossibility, for example – but I can neither deny nor fail to take into consideration, in my becoming, the relationship with the other gender which goes with belonging to my own. To be woman necessarily involves – as far as human essence and existence are concerned – to be in relationship with man, at least ontologically. Supposing that this is even possible.

In fact, I am created by two genders and I live in a mixed community. But let us consider a utopia of our age: a woman gives birth to a woman, and they live in a community of women separated from the other part of the world. A woman in such a situation should consider her identity as woman as an identity in relationship with the other gender, at least in so far as it is her intention to fulfill her own gender. There is in me, woman, a part which is negative, not realizable by me alone, a part of night, a part which is reserved, a part which is irreducibly feminine and which is not suited to represent the whole of the human being that must enter into the constitution of my identity.

Perhaps it is up to women to think it. They, who generate in themselves the other gender, can perhaps better conceive the two of subjectivity, of gender, and not only the one.

This two does not allow the submission of one to the other, if it is not to suffer the loss of the two. It does not even correspond to a juxtaposition of one+one subjects. It has to do with a relationship *between*.

This relationship between the two genders cannot be reduced to passivity for the female and activity for the male,[a] as still happens in our tradition with such philosophers as Sartre, Merleau-Ponty, and Lévinas. This division annuls one's own identity: the two genders, the two people in relationship with each other no longer remain. They have become two ways of being man and woman: more lover or more beloved, more active or more passive, more gazing or more seen-visible. One way of being is not enough to constitute an identity. Instead, it paralyzes the interiority involved in receiving a partial destination and function determined by the existence of the other who is without a proper intentionality.

Being passive or active – in oneself and between oneself – are ways of being that are used by Sartre to qualify the relationships between the in-itself and the for-itself of consciousness: it is persecutor or persecuted, as are even the "concrete" relations with the other: the subject is looker or looked upon, seer or seen.

What Sartre desires is that the other makes himself an in-itself, or rather object-objecticity for me the subject, while I still transform myself into an ideal and absolute in-itself for him. I would thus become the visible ideal by which his gaze allows itself to be fascinated.

Desire for the other as other does not seem to interest Sartre. "I love you and desire you because you fulfill the becoming of your gender, that which is inscribed in your body" does not hold his attention. Nor does the desire for the other as carnally other, nor the attraction towards him as a being different from me, with an existence irreducible to mine, seem to be his. The fact that I can look at the other, contemplate him as body and as thought, does not concern him. The other remains the one whom I fear as the cause of my alienation, of my decline, of my fall into factuality, into the sensibility of incarnation.

What does sexual liberation mean if the relationship with the other remains conceived in these terms? Does it involve an even greater destruction of the other's consciousness?

Desire for the other, in so far as it is tied to the consciousness of his own body and, in another way, to his own history, is not yet considered a philosophical question either by Sartre or by the latest Western philosophers. Desire for me, woman, as a different consciousness, proper to the body of another gender, remains a blindspot in their minds. Even today, the confrontation of these ontological problems is not recognized by the majority as a philosophical task. This dimension of the human being should remain relegated to an uncultivated empiricism. True, many things and many interests intervene in such a change in the limits of thought and of its nature! Touching them means risking clashes fraught with misunderstandings, with censures that are more or less voluntary and, more radically, with a consciousness which has not been thought in its to be, incarnated in and by its own body.

If a gesture of this sort were to take place, philosophy would have to recognize that two subjects exist and that reason must measure itself against the reality and the to be of those two subjects, in their horizontal and vertical dimensions.

Philosophy would, therefore, be refounded upon the existence of two different subjects and not upon the one, the singular, the same. This would involve a sort of revolution in thought directed towards an anticapitalism of spirituality, towards an acceptance that consciousness, truth, and ideality are two. A two of this kind would not be"turbid", "double", "equivocal", "ambiguous", terms used by some philosophers when they speak of a relation between two subjects in which each one loses his or her irreducibility.

Such a revolution in thought would permit the constitution of an interiority different from that determined by and destined to a transcendence of the beyond or constituted within a genealogical order: a respect for parents, a cult of ancestors, a love for one's children. This new interiority could exist only in the sphere of a sexuate relationship: since I am not you, I can open a space of interiority in me.

The limit which derives from belonging to a gender is not only a limit to my presence: in the world, in my encounter with the other, with others; it is also a limit which delineates a horizon of interiority. Because I am not you, I can return within myself, collect myself, think. Without this limit, consciousness can be reduced to the "pursuit of an impossible future", as Sartre says; it can be placed in search of an autistic absolute, corresponding both to a singular subject and to a people, and can expand towards a transcendence situated beyond the one who thinks, in the direction of an in-finite space or time. From the moment that I am not you, every instant allows me to return to myself. You are the one who helps me to remain in myself, to stay in myself, to contain or keep me in myself, to remain present and not paralyzed by the past or in flight towards the future. Your irreducible alterity gives me the present, presence: the possibility of being in myself, of attempting to cultivate the in-stasy and not only the ex-stasy.

Entering or being in the presence of two who are different does not, therefore, involve reduction to factuality or to "facticity", but the possibility of returning to myself, in the recognition of the irreducible difference between woman and man. This pause in front of the other returns me to the present, to presence. This coming to a stop in front of the other is recognition, but it is also a desire and appeal to overcome the interval which separates us.

We have a way of doing it: the way of instinct, of the drives, of sexual attraction, but this path deceives us most of the time We lose ourselves in its simple pursuit. Supposing that the inclination persists, repeats itself, another way is still needed so that it can be elaborated and that we can build a relationship between us, between two.

In order to avoid the interval, the irreducible separation between us, in most cases we produce children and create familial senti-ments from their desire.

Others, or perhaps the same ones, build intellectual construc-tions which claim to overcome the sensible.

Perhaps we also find consolation in the belief in an afterlife, which sometimes absolves us from having to work on happiness here below.

We have not yet cultivated our attraction towards each other, above all together, between two. From *I Love to You* onwards, I have attempted to perform such a task. Within my intentions there is a desire to overcome the immediate inclination between us, thus preserving both the energy and the between-two. For this reason, I am attempting to propose relationships between two which are more human, more pleasing, that is, a life here on earth where there is greater happiness.

The will to change the relations between men and women cannot simply limit itself to a relationship between two, to dia-logue. It is necessary to privilege some of these relations: encounters between woman and man take place which, simultaneously, represent an event that allows for the constitution of interiority and a task to be performed. Furthermore, this way of linking myself to the other protects me from the alienation and fascination produced by the fabricated, "manufactured" world which surrounds us, preventing a communal between-us.

Several words provided by Sartre on the constitution of the we-subject make this difficulty apparent.

As soon as I use a manufactured object, I meet upon it the outline of my own transcendence; it indicates to me the movement to be made; I am to turn, push, draw, or lean. Moreover we are dealing here with an hypothetical imperative; it refers me to an end which is equally in the world: *if* I want to sit down, *if* I want to open the box, etc. And this end has been anticipated in the constitution of the object as an end posited by some transcendence.[b] It belongs at present to the object as its most peculiar potentiality. Thus it is true that the manufactured object makes me known to myself as "they"; that is, it refers me to the image of my transcendence as that of any transcendence whatsoever.[c] And if I allow my possibilities to be channeled by the instrument thus constituted, I experience myself as any transcendence:[d] to go from the subway station at "Trocadéro" to "Sèvres-Babylone," "They" change at "La Motte-Picquet." This change is foreseen, indicated on maps, etc.; if I change routes at La Motte-Picquet, I am the "They" who change. To be sure, I differentiate myself by each use of the subway as much by the individual upsurge of my being as by the distant ends which I pursue. But these final ends are only on the horizon of my act. My immediate ends are the ends of the "They", and I apprehend myself as interchangeable with any one of my neighbors. In this sense we lose our real individuality, for the project which we are is precisely the project which others are. In this subway corridor there is only one and the same project, inscribed a long time ago in matter, where a living and undifferentiated transcendence[e] comes to be absorbed. To the extent that I realize myself in solitude as any transcendence,[f] I have only the experience of undifferentiated-being (e.g. if alone in my room I open a bottle of preserves with the proper bottle opener). But if this undifferentiated transcendence[g] projects its projects, whatever they are, in connection with other transcendences experienced as real presences similarly absorbed in projects identical with my projects, then I realize my project as one among thousands of identical projects projected by one and the same undifferentiated transcendence.[h]. Then I have the experience of a common transcendence directed toward a unique end of which I am only an ephemeral particularization; I insert myself into the great human stream which from the time that the subway first existed has flowed incessantly into the corridors of the station"La Motte-Picquet-Grenelle."[1]

Participating in a social or cultural movement can create different types of empathy, sympathy, and solidarity between individuals; but they are generally determined beginning from the exteriority of the shared world, and they are not born from me. The environment causes me to be like everyone else, to do as they do, to find solidarity with them rather than to affirm my singularity. For this reason, I am not attentive to the other, to others, but do as they do through passivity, through egoism, I would say.

I, thus, become an "any body" which only my intention towards you can help me to overcome.

I am not reduced to an "any body" in the corridor of the subway station at La Motte-Picquet-Grenelle if I walk towards you. My interiority, my intention, remain my own in spite of the crowd. This interiority of mine safeguards my mystery as your interiority leaves you a mystery for me.

I am protected from the transcendence of the "any body" in three ways:

I am sexuate, I am not neuter, anonymous or interchangeable;

I am animated by my intentions towards the other, in particular towards you, and not simply determined by the world which surrounds me;

I am a mystery for you, as you are for me, and our intersubjectivity is protected from the imperative originating in the exterior world and in the anonymity of its destination addressed to an "any body".

4

To perceive the invisible in you

Objects as such, whether concrete or abstract, sensible or mental, are not necessary for perception. I can perceive another living being while still respecting him as subject. This corresponds to an objectual perception with a something extra which remains foreign to simple objective reduction, a something extra which is left to the other: a history, a becoming, an interiority.

To sensation are related the object and its properties, its origin, and its concrete or abstract cause.

When the relationship with the other is reduced to sensation, to simple affect, the other, even if he is active, becomes an object, losing his qualities as subject. In a conception of sexuality centered upon instinct, drives, affect, the partners,[a] men and women, come to be defined as either the haves or have-nots of corporeal "objects" capable of producing and experiencing _jouissance_. They are no extreme happiness longer considered subjects. Interpreted in such an instrumental manner, sexuality is left uncultivated, or rather, assimilated to a techne which does not take intersubjectivity into account.

technique

Perception implies: I am not you, you are irreducible to me. The one who looks and the one who is looked upon cannot be substituted for each other, and not just in this active-passive relationship. They do not look in the same manner. They look at each other between each other.

If I look at myself in the mirror, if I see the other in the mirror, perception resembles sensation. The image reflected by the mirror, or by the mind, has lost the volume of the body; I see myself in only two dimensions, and I see the other as an inverted _alter ego_.

While this spectacle sometimes arouses jubilation, it is often a question of death or of murder. In any event, the relationship between two is avoided, because it reduces me and the other to an image. But this avoidance does not occur without the production of aggression, of hatred, and it does not permit the construction of love. In the mirror I can become an other, I can seek the Other, I can reduce the other to my perspective: we are never two. Artifice has annihilated the relationship between the two subjects.

We are dealing, to a certain extent, with the same process which takes place in the reduction of everyone to equality. An invisible mirror erases the living identity of each person and paralyzes the fecundity of the relations between them. This "ideal" resembles in some ways the zero of sexual tensions discussed by Freud; but this model, taken up again by the sciences of the non-living, neutralizes the lives of people as individuals or as communities.

Whereas perception seems to be fitting for life, sensation seems more a path towards death. Cultivating perception means being attentive to the qualities both of what is perceived and of the one who perceives. The economy of sensation is more quantitative than qualitative: feeling always wants to grow in intensity and continues along this path until death due to the lack of any controls. In fact, the sadist and the masochist play with death.

Between two living beings, sensibility fluctuates, if it is faithful to perception. The other changes, and I also change. If you remain alive, my gaze, my senses are always aroused by your present intentions, and I cannot fall asleep in my knowledge of you, in the repetition of what I have already felt from you, as long as a stronger sensation keeps me awake. Your gestures, if they are inspired by your desire, attract my attention, my gaze. Its horizon is not closed but remains open upon your mystery, upon the irreducibility of your freedom, upon your intention. Turned towards you, my eyes are centered upon you, but they do not yet have, within, an image or a spectacle. They are always and already virginal when looking at you, at the expression of your desire. But if you are not animated by anything, if you mime or repeat a model, a role, my gaze will be preoccupied and fundamentally altered, it will lack interest in its present and in its future and will no longer be nourished by them. It will remain only stained by what is visible and without possible intentionality or interiorization, held back and enchanted by an incomprehensible nothing: neither subject nor object.

Where can I rest my gaze? Where, if not upon you, animated by a spiritual intention which does not exclude me, by a project which attempts to unite heaven and earth? Not until I rest it upon the nature which surrounds me does it give me life and testimony of growth.

In love, the gaze often remains fascination, enchantment, occasionally rape and possession. Why is it that the other who looks at me during or after loving can injure me? He looks at an object, not at a subject. He is unfaithful to an intention, to an interiority, to a gaze which we can share.

Perhaps loving each other requires that we look at the invisible together, that we abandon the sight of it to the breath of the heart, of the soul, that we preserve it in its carnality, without staring upon it fixedly as a target.

A body that is in love does not endure being fixed as an object. Cutting it out of space and time destroys that carnal immersion required by a loving relationship. Intimate relations become a way of tearing at the lovers, a cutting of their bodies, of their spirits, of their rhythms and of the cosmic rhythms in which the sensibility of love participates.

Love involves all of the senses, including sight and sound. But looking at a precise objective and looking at the other with respect for his intention and his interiority are quite different things.

Our spiritual senses are not trained to love. We do not yet know how to look at or listen to the other as subject. We still ignore the possibility of giving up a centered gaze, a fixed sight, a renunciation which would leave space and air around and within the other. I look at someone who, to a certain degree, remains invisible to me. I refuse the separation between the visible of this world and the invisible of the beyond. I look at you who are invisible against a background of invisibility: a background composed of our interiorities, our becomings.

I look at you as at the passage of the word into flesh, of the flesh into word, a lasting incarnation, the fulfillment of which is not perceptible by whoever does not keep his or her gaze upon the invisible.

In my perception of you, in this "mine" which you have become through my perception, struck by you, I must free myself from appropriation. Certainly I, woman, look at you, love you and perhaps think of you, but what I perceive, love and think about, is not mine. A negative prevents your reduction to me, in me. I will never be you, you will never be mine. A gap remains between me and you, between you and me. I will never be capable of perceiving you completely, and not even of loving you, or of speaking to you completely.

To escape this impossibility, men have created an absolute which is inaccessible, which is completely other with respect to us.

But the absolutely inaccessible other is, above all, here and now between us. We are incapable of being substituted in body or mind, in perceptions, affects, judgments, etc.

Perceiving you does not involve losing me or you, as long as I accept that this perception is not simply mine. It is mine and not mine. My body perceives in a manner which is more or less correct, but my spirit does not allow for appropriation: my perception must remain a path towards you, towards us, an us which is always disunited, distanced, always a "two" irreducible to one.

Perception should not become a means of appropriating the other, of abstracting the body, but should be cultivated for itself, without being reduced to a passivity or to an activity of the senses. It can correspond to the elaboration of the sensible through the mental, and vice versa. Sensation, on the other hand, is sustained by a passive affect, with a subjective participation tied to its intensity, to its more or less pleasing character.

While perception can assist in the construction of intersubjectivity, sensation tends to erase one of the two subjects or reduce them both to a game between forces that are more or less individuated and controlled.

Thanks to perception, we can each become, the one for the other, a bridge towards a becoming which is yours, mine, and ours. I can be a bridge for you, as you can be one for me. This bridge can never become the property of either. The bridge which I am for you will never be mine or "to me". I perceive you, I create an idea of you, I preserve you in my memory – in affect, in thought – in order to assist you in your becoming. While I become me, I remember you.

This should be a double gesture: you should be a bridge for me, as I should be one for you.

Without a doubt, these bridges are not the same. A double passage must intervene in our exchanges, the two being necessary for the protection of intersubjectivity. Lacking this double memory, each one speaks of him or herself – assuming that this "self" really exists – expressing wishes and sensations, manifesting an ideology for which he or she is only the authoritarian mouthpiece in the absence of intersubjectivity.

Authority is never clearly represented in a person, even if this person conveys it or acts as its agent. One problem with our era is that we denounce the tyrants of the past while remaining unaware of the tyrannical ideology which circulates between us.

Against the power of such an ideology, of which everyone and no one is the vehicle, it seems useful to return to the objective criteria of sensibility, for example those present in perception.

In order to facilitate the relations between subjects, perception must be cultivated by memory and also by the rigor of thought.

Clearly, safeguarding corresponds to a spiritual gesture. Remembering, without holding anything back for oneself, is even more of a spiritual gesture. Would it not resemble a movement along a path for which we still lack words? Would it not, perhaps, be the way along which to cultivate breathing, the breath, and perhaps also to sublimate the instincts and affection between us?

Perception is sensibility, but it does not confuse the body with the soul, the work of the senses with the work of thought. Sensation would like to join them together, but before or without the cultivation of perception. Such a conception of the sensible would allow for the reduction of each and every subject to a single subjectivity: a human, universal, abstract, asexuate subject. In so far as he is collective, the subject is placed under a single order and, in so far as he is singular, he is kept outside the present, outside presence. In each case, the subject remains abstract, the fruit of an alienating constitution. Understood in this way, sensation paralyzes the spiritual becoming of the breath, its present presence, its sensible culture, its safeguarding at the service of the subject, of the world, of the other.

Sensation overturns perception in the night of the soul, reducing it to passivity towards the already established order. In contrast, perception remains aroused by what presents itself. It cultivates the attention required to discern reality, truth, love, the world, and other things as they are rather than as I imagine or would like them to be. Sensation remains more blindly passive in what is felt, and does not discriminate between dream, artifice and what is real or true.

Perceiving, if it is cultivated as such, is part of becoming together. Sensation, instead, loses the other, even the world: it takes pleasure in them but without remaining with them, and thus forms an atemporal being, or rather, a being for whom time unfolds only beginning from the intensity of experience,[b] above all, of suffering. The subject remains alone with the history of his affections, of his sensations, a history which he remembers, recounts, and repeats. The subject does not construct an active temporality, a temporality-with, but becomes reactive, saturated with intensity, without freedom, without space for initiative or creation.

In listening to the other, to the world, perception must remain the form of present sensibility, unless I listen to nothing or no one, and project upon others or impose upon them only what I am. When sensation prevails in the encounter with the other or with the world, sensibility becomes an exercise of power and submission. In being-with, in being-together, there are those who are capable of manipulating sensation and those who simply submit themselves to it in a blind manner. Any relationship puts power into play, unless it is reduced to the submission of a third: an already existing creation, culture, truth.

Approaching the other requires perceiving him as other. Thus, the other remains a living subject, perceived in his becoming and, if I can put it this way, his appearance is not separated from his matter, nor is it a fabrication which is foreign to his reality.

When perception – of the world, of the other, of language, of thought – is in error, there is an imbalance between their form and substance. At that point, perception is supplanted by sensation. Association, in this case, can be immediate and more intense, but it is still passive, artificial and outside the constitution of a temporality which does not involve the exercise of one's power over the other. If it gives rise to affection, association does not arouse thought; rather, it causes reason to regress and, what is more, it brings about a loss of energy. All of this carries with it the risk of alienating the spirit in the rules and regulations of power exercised by those masters who are as authoritarian as they are incompetent.

To respect you requires that, in my perception of you, I do not limit myself to the merely felt, that I refuse to be only moved by you.

Your appearance to me requires a distance, a perspective which maintains the two. Approaching you along a path which is solely phenomenal is not enough to establish an ethical relationship between us. It imposes a dialectic between each of our appearances.

A certain amount of method is required in order to remove both me and you, or us, from the passivity of perception. For example, what moves one of my senses can be found in the ensemble of my perceptions of you and, thus, can lead – both you and me – towards an idea of you, a thought about you, a respect for you, much like a path which goes from the outside to the inside of you and, in a different manner, of me.

What captures my attention can teach me how to sustain your becoming, how to approach you, how to dialogue with you. What moves me can give rise to praise, to grace, to admiration.

I cannot make immediate use of what I receive from you without referring it back to you: for instance, I cannot use your image solely to be seduced by it. I must not appropriate what you suggest to my sensibility without having an intention for you in myself. A dialectic between us is necessary, so that each may exist in his or her appearance, in his or her fulfillment, in his or her being and to be in a manner which is perceptible to the senses of the other's being and to be. What you bring to my perceptions cannot enter into the constitution of my to be without reference to, memory of, or a contribution to your to be.

To leave the other to be, not to possess him in any way, to contemplate him as an irreducible presence, to relish him as an inappropriable good, to see him, to listen to him, to touch him, knowing that what I perceive is not mine. Sensed by me, yet remaining other, never reduced to an object. Received without anyone renouncing him or herself, if not in the abandonment of being looked after by the other. Almost no trace of exteriority exists in such sharing, apart from a faithful memory and, perhaps, an alliance.

To respect you: to perceive you through the senses, leaving an extra cloud of invisibility. I perceive you, but what I perceive is not the whole of you, and the whole of me is not perception. I perceive what is already apparent. I perceive it with my eyes, my ears, my nose, my touch, my taste. What can I say of what is not perceptible in this manner? What I feel in excess of it – to whom does this belong?

Perceiving you is a way of approaching us, an encounter in the distance, made possible thanks to our senses. What remains to be considered is what I perceive and what I offer to be perceived. What remains to be given is a perspective to perspective itself. What remains to be established is a relationship between the you which exists in space and the you which exists in my thoughts, in my heart. What remains to be given is a spiritual measure to my sensibility, as if I were looking at you with one eye and evaluating you with the other. When the gaze can be harmonized in one, I contemplate you, and I contemplate in you the union of your corporeal and spiritual natures.

You, therefore, allow me to see the invisible. The invisible is here. You are visible and invisible. In you, the invisible appears but also remains collected, quiet, calm. It appears and exists.

It is not necessary to enter the beyond in order to find pleasure in it: it is enough to contemplate you, to think of you. It is like the sky which gives itself and withdraws itself, near and distant, always other.

I who am visible to you must also protect a certain reserve. Within the intention of appearing to you, there must also exist the intention of remaining invisible, of covering life and love with the shadow of a secret. The eyes are a bridge between us, the gestures express a desire, but this shows itself by hiding itself.

Thus, I am clothed even when I am naked. My body is never reduced to a simple naturality: the desire to loveᶜ always and already weaves a cloak made both by me and by you, made of earth and of sky, of night and of light, of shadow and of sun. And thus to infinity.

5

To love to the point of safeguarding you

In us, passages between perceptions and sensations are habitual. For example:

I perceive the other and lose myself when perception becomes sensation;

I perceive the other and make this perception an object of my affection: for me, perception remains an excess of sensation;

I perceive the other and am estranged in him or her, or I estrange the other in me: by not respecting perception, I erase the two.

This reduction of the two to the one subjects perception to simple feeling.

There are many consequences which follow from a gesture of this sort. The sensible of perception is not cultivated according to the order of reason or the order of communication. It falls back into sensation, into what favors the constitution of a subject who is as universal as he is solitary. Indeed, many qualities of sensation can be imagined as universal: the taste of food, the smell of flowers, the sight of colors, the experience of cold and hot, sexual attraction ... Although it is not certain that sensation is universal, common to everyone, we still believe it to be so because it is transmitted through a series of communications and encounters, in a language which is defined in an abstract, neuter, and insensible way – all in the name of universality.

Perceiving can never be made universal, at least in the sense that perception remains tied to the singularity of an encounter, of a being in presence. As such, it is not possible to assimilate it to models which can be separated from the present.

In perceiving the other, if I annul the gap and the difference between us, I become the other and make him mine. We are no longer two. Perception is abolished in sensation or in a representational scheme which forgets the real presence between us. I perceive myself beginning from my sense of the other and I perceive him within the horizon of my history, of my affections, including those which are intellectual. The becoming of each finds itself paralyzed as a result of the abolition of perception between the two, a perception which is always different and always new.

There is a need to construct a temporal becoming of this kind of perception by remembering the present, the encounter in presence, the perception in presence, the present presence.

If I become the other – through love, for example – I abolish the two poles I – you, she – he. Thus, the relationship between two disappears and, with it, a possible dialogue and a possible intersubjective dialectic. Reality becomes a dream or a sensation and forgets about external reality, in particular the other's external reality. In this way, a fictitious interiority grows.

The historical construction of our subjectivity makes possible this becoming in the unreality of a dream. I lose the return to myself, the respect for the other, and the intersubjective relationship.

Becoming the other without returning within myself is part of such a dream. It corresponds to an inertia, to an imaginary creation, to a becoming that loses the way back: to the self, to one's own perceptions, to presence in the world, to the other.

Such becoming annuls communication-between. If I become what captures my attention, what I desire, I do not protect my relationship with the world, with the other. My desire abolishes its three constituent terms: the one who desires, the one who is desired, and desire itself. Perceiving has become feeling, at times in the form of ecstasy. I, the perceived, the relationship between me and the world, between me and the other, are confused in a sensation which does not protect our respective identities: all that remains is the I who suffers, the I who feels good, the I who delights in myself.

When sensation is pleasant, it inspires longing and appropriation. If it is unpleasant, it provokes flight, contempt, and rejection.

Sensation does not necessarily help my growth, but brings with it the loss of my sensoriality, of my perception of the other, of my becoming together with him.

A culture of sensation such as ours involves a becoming of subjectivity which is, in part, blind: when laying the foundations of the felt, when establishing thought, it does not concern itself with the world, the other, others. I mistakenly think that I can raise myself above the sensible in order to overcome all that I believe is inferior to the intellect. I realize this gesture in a manner which is solitary and solipsistic.

The sensible, therefore, is considered as a sensation or an affect not cultivated as such, in particular in the relationship between two. We remain in an infantile state of feeling: I have experienced, I want what I have experienced; I do not ask myself from whom or from what that which I have felt comes. It is reduced to a cause of appetite, of appropriation – oral or anal, as Freud would say –, to an occasion for suffering if the object is lacking, to a reason for decline or regression.

Sensibility is maintained at the level of the untrained senses, of the elementary instincts. Perceiving does not become an occasion for cultivation, for thought: it is annulled in sensation.

Another path is possible. For example, perception can be trained as a spiritual method. As such, it becomes a means for respecting what exists, for contemplating it and achieving an ecstasy/in-stasy in the relationship with the perceived. This can take place in the contemplation of nature: I am thinking about the gaze of Buddha towards the flower, as well as the attention paid by many spiritualists to the songs of the birds.

Abolishing the distinction between subject and object does not seem to me to be the end of this journey, as several masters from the Far East would have it (Patañjali, for example). Although it leads to ecstasy, such a gesture appears to me to be an annulment both of the "subject" and of the "object", an annulment desired by these masters.

I, woman, prefer to contemplate nature, the other, as they can be contemplated and, through contemplation, to cultivate my subjectivity, my energy, thanks to perception itself. Subjectivity, therefore, arrives at spirituality while remaining sensibility.

Beginning from this point, perception can become a practice at the service of intersubjective relationships. The cultivation of my perception requires a partial renunciation of immediate sensibility. In perceiving the other as other, it is necessary to distinguish who perceives from what or who is perceived. Certainly we are no longer merely in a relationship between a subject and an object;

we are also dealing with a relationship between two subjects, the objective of which is to leave to the other his or her subjectivity.

This intersubjective culture is still missing, and we always fall back into the subject/object dichotomy and, in more general terms, into the logic of binary oppositions: hot/cold, active/passive, masculine/feminine, with sensibility no longer a feeling between present subjects, but a kind of experience in which a subject is reduced to an "object" which arouses or experiences sensation.

When I perceive the other, it is important that I am attentive to at least three dimensions: the qualities of the subject who perceives, the other present to me as an object of perception, the other who is and must remain a subject.

In perception, I can individuate the one who perceives: for example, I am a woman and, as such, I am interested in one kind of perception more than in another, and I perceive in a specific manner.

These modalities participate in my perception, in which this other that I am for myself intervenes, unknown to me; for instance, by revealing to me several characteristics of my gender.

But, if I perceive another subject, I must also leave him or her his or her alterity. This appears in an obvious manner when the other is of a gender different from my own. In fact, in the act of perceiving, I cannot substitute myself for him, and I must respect in the perception which I have of the other the irreducibility of his gender. I perceive the other and I must, in some way, give back to him an inverted perspective of what I perceive. If I must protect the singularity of my perspective in order to remain a subject in perception, I must likewise leave, return, and give to the other his perspective.

It can happen that this other who remains, in part, unimaginable to me in his subjectivity becomes mine through an illusion: through an immediate perception or sensation. But this "mine" is never really "mine", and if I make it such on account of an illusory appropriation, I renounce my subjectivity. This "mine" names a mistaken interiority: it is maintained between exteriority and interiority like a question without an answer. If I fail to ask the question, I abolish the gap which makes intersubjectivity possible for me.

In the relationship between two subjects, in the constitution of intersubjectivity, one must take into account a nothingness in common – "an almost absolute silence", as I wrote in *I Love to You* – in order to begin to speak to each other.

This nothingness in common, furthermore, permits the constitution of a free interiority in which the other, because he is not mine, remains mobile in me, an energy tied to him but free between us: an energy linked by an inclination and by a "not".

This "not" is double, but it is different as far as you and I are concerned. What I perceive of you is not me, and is not even you. But this "not" takes away the energy and the to be from the immobility and inertia of being, which is found in the very horizon of death.

Between us, it is possible that the to be will never become being thanks to a suspension or an ascesis of energy itself. If we are to delineate our human to be, the irreducibility between us must be substituted for the necessity of death. Once this is accomplished, each of us would be allowed to be or to enter into the presence of the other, something which is impossible in a horizon where death is the absolute mistress.

In the absence of a "not", in immediate affection towards the other as well as in blind faith in him, the to be closes itself in the form of being. It might be that this is necessary, in order to avoid the loss of energy in its entirety, but it should remain a pause, a hypothesis for safeguarding this energy and what already exists in the journey towards the other. For this reason, it cannot be confused with finality: it must remain a protection against regression to the infinite. Thus, my faith in you cannot erase the difference and the "not" between us. There must always exist a questioning towards you in so far as you are a being, and towards me, in so far as I am capable or incapable of a to be.

Up to now, we have not succeeded in making the space around us and between us temporal. We speak beginning from the exteriority of things, and not beginning from interiority. We communicate at the level of needs, of objects, of spatial configurations – forms, perspectives, movements, displacements. We still lack the knowledge necessary to interiorize the to be present to each other, and the knowledge necessary to interiorize the relationship between us.

We can realize this stage of our human becoming beginning

from our own body, from this living interiority which is imperceptible to each one of us as such.

We perceive, think, and remember the encounter between living bodies through different types of particularity: colors, height, age, facial features, health, etc. We have not considered this encounter within the horizon of what is, at the same time, interior and exterior to us, of what unites the in-us with the outside-of-us: gender.

Intersubjectivity, in order to succeed in interiorizing the exteriority of the human, must take into account the dimension of gender as a means capable of protecting alterity.

6

I announce to you that we are different

The mystery of the Annunciation, like the devotion of Antigone, are two moments that must be examined in order to interpret our tradition.

Rethinking the announcement made to Mary within the cultural horizon of the Far East, in particular that of the *chakras*, illuminates this event in a new way.

It can, thus, become an experience of love for everyone. Moreover, it can be understood as a reciprocal revelation which woman and man can give to each other, as much in words as at the level of sensible perception and of energetic fecundity, directed towards a spiritual journey which is singular and common.

According to the texts of these traditions, the master teaches his disciple to cultivate his energy. Even today, in the teachings of yoga, for example, one deals more with a cultivation of energy than with a transmission of theoretical knowledge. Doubtless, it is helpful to have access to the words of past masters, but practice itself remains the principle medium of these teachings. It aspires to dispel all forms of suffering and of aging, to rediscover infancy, to be reborn. Perhaps the words of Jesus: "If you do not become like these little children, you will not enter the Kingdom of Heaven" testify that he was an initiate of yoga, a tradition of energy and of interiority.

The practitioner of yoga must proceed in his life in a way which has been forgotten by us: he does not have to accept the weight of the years, he does not have to believe that wisdom is an accumulation of knowledge, or that the man who has suffered is necessarily a good master. Instead, he must learn to cultivate his energy until he arrives at a reawakening – remaining innocent, virgin in spirit – always becoming more alive and younger.

Such teachings are presented in the form of a transmission from a master to a disciple. To a certain degree, this resembles a parental and genealogical education, a form of assistance given to children to aid their growth.

Fidelity to one's own gender opens the way to another becoming: a becoming woman, a becoming man, a becoming together.

If the energy of each moves in a different manner, if they have a different relationship to sounds and colors, perhaps they can teach these differences to each other, each being simultaneously – as man and woman – master and disciple for the other. Each, faithful to him or herself, would bring to the other his or her own energy and his or her manner of cultivating it . This practice would not be able to be appropriated by the other. Energy must be received without asserting dominion over its production. If it becomes mine, if I want to appropriate it, I lose it. If I receive, I receive it, respecting it as the other's. It allows me to be with an extra amount of energy.

This is unthinkable according to our logic. Indeed, this "mystery" announces itself once a particular path has been forgotten, the path of an amorous knowledge which is as spiritual as it is carnal.

For example, Aristotle teaches that woman is cold while man is hot. We still live the relationship between the genders in this way: woman should be warmed by man; she should seduce him in order to be warmed by him, rekindled by him.

But in this case, difference is envisioned only from the outside and in a way which is dichotomous. The tradition of the Far East teaches us that woman is hot inside and cold outside, while man is cold inside and hot outside. If this is true, man can point out to the woman who is faithful to herself the way back to the source of her energy: hot, while woman can allow man to return to his: cold.

Something very similar happens with colors. For instance, blue is often attributed to the feminine and red to the masculine. But this is only valid at the level of appearance: the feminine manifests itself as blue beginning from the red, and the masculine as red beginning from the blue.

And the very same thing happens with sounds: lower or higher, more physical or more mental, hotter or colder, more masculine or more feminine.

Being attentive to these differences involves both respect for the other and fidelity to one's own gender. Lacking such attentiveness, I seek my hot depths in the hot exteriority of the other and, rather than returning to the heat within myself, I search for it outside of myself and never find it.

Once this is taken into account, it is preferable to make woman into the one who loves, and not only into the one who is loved. Loving is heat, and loving, for woman, implies taking care of her own heat. It is a way of being faithful to the heat within her.

We, on the other hand, are accustomed to living the difference between the genders through two types of exteriority: woman seeks herself in man, who, in turn, seeks himself in the mother.

In order to escape this infernal circle, logic has imagined an original causality, philosophy has imagined the univocal nature of truth, and our religious tradition – sustained by dogmas which fix the evolution of faith – has imagined the authority of a God-Father.

But my causality cannot be reduced to an authority which is singular and solely exterior to me; it is also an interiority which takes difference (differences) as its point of departure.

My parents represent an origin which is external to me, at least in the dimension of genealogy. They are at the origin of me. Maturity would consist in becoming the cause of and for oneself, in giving oneself an origin which is one's own. This is the objective put forward by the masters of the Far East.

There is another way: a way which recognizes that what determines me, what is the cause of and for me, belongs partly to the other, to the other of sexual difference in particular. My life as woman, the interiority which I also receive from the other-man, is made fecund and grows beginning from the encounter between I-woman and you-man if we are each faithful to our own gender.

The other becomes the light and the heat which illuminate me, which make new possibilities spring forth in me, with faithfulness to myself being the root, stem and trunk for this becoming.

From this perspective, a single origin does not exist, nor is there an origin common to many: a *logos*, a civilization, a religious or civil authority. We do not belong only to a family, to a people, to a nation, to a culture. Singular and multiple origins, different genealogies exist for me, for us and between us. I am born in/of a family, in a determinate period of History, in a precise place and within the context of a tradition. But I have encountered and crossed other causalities. And it happens this way for everyone. Together, we represent many differences which are more or less compatible.

Desire can keep us together, can reunite us. But, although it is as old as the world, this way of mediating communitarian life has not been understood. The nostalgia of the one has always supplanted desire between two.[a]

This nostalgia takes different paths. It can aspire to fusion: with nature, with a divine figure, with the energy of the other, others. At times, it corresponds to the self-love of Narcissus. Often, it is equivalent to the desire to be or to possess the whole.

To remain between two requires the renunciation of this sort of unity: fusional, regressive, autistic, narcissistic.

To abide between two is to accept the fact that the whole can never be reached either through progression or regression, annihilation or possession.

To be as two allows for the construction of History, for the cultivation of humanity in its incompleteness, in its non-dominion, and also in the happiness of its shared energy, in the joy of a path that is taken together.

To maintain the two is to give up the sort of infancy which places the omnipotent parental One above, as well as the familial relationship which returns it below. This preservation of the two also requires the maturity to give up the needs of childhood and to renounce parental power.

To be two means to help each other to be, to discover and to cultivate happiness, to take care of the difference between us, not merely because of its role in generation, because it represents the means of humanity's production and reproduction, but in order to achieve happiness and make it blossom.

Along this path, woman can be a guide for man because, born of one similar to herself, she is more capable of a relationship between subjects, and the subject-object duality is not as much a part of her subjectivity as it is a part of man's.

But, in order to guide the other, she must renounce fusion, submission, possession. Where man seeks the one, overcoming the scission between subject and object, woman must learn to remain two. Woman must be the one to initiate this process of remaining two, two who are differentiated, but not according to the mother-child, mother-son model. In order to do this, she must gain her own autonomy, her own interiority.

For centuries, woman has appeared as superficiality itself – save for the natural profundity which is in the service of love and, above all, in the service of maternity, that is, physical interiority. She has been considered fickle, capricious, the one to whom thought and interiority always remain foreign. To make man come out of himself, to awaken him from his dreams, she is asked to attract him in the game of seduction and love.

There is, perhaps, an historical origin to this feminine "destiny". It is born in the era which demands that woman be clothed while man remains nude. Perhaps it corresponds to the passage from matriarchy to patriarchy, or rather from carnal love, of which woman is goddess, to phallocracy. Athena and Apollo are figures-traces of this transition.

As a result, it seems that woman's garment becomes more important than her skin. It appears to be forgotten that women are more spiritual than men, beginning from this corporeal fabric which is genetically tied to the mental.

Privileging the garment conceals a place of the spiritual to be for the feminine. In fact, endeavoring to be pretty in appearance through the use of artifice means, for woman, renouncing the spirituality of her skin, a spirituality which is more human and mental than man's.

The caress which causes woman to fall into a state of infancy, of animality, of perversity, and which returns man to his "God", diverts woman from her spiritual destiny. Man appropriates it, and gains a part of its energy, which he uses to pursue his own way.

From that moment, the spiritual becoming of each is altered, perverted. Woman falls into the absence of intellect and thought, and man builds his culture beginning from the submission and appropriation of the other, but does not, as man, become spiritual. His spirit remains dominion, possession, capture, and not a path towards masculine interiority.

When the caress is not a call for each person to return within him or herself, to his or her own interiority, when, for woman, it is not a reawakening to communication, mental or otherwise, it is a corrupt gesture whose guilt must be assigned to man, or to both man and woman.

As Buddha has taught, it would be better if each man attempted to awaken his own skin. Renouncing possession and all forms of ownership which fragment becoming in relationship with the object, Buddha breathes and even laughs, with all of his skin.

The attention we have paid to such teachings is still inadequate, failing as we do to cultivate it together. If we were more attentive, we would be flowers capable of opening ourselves to the light of the sun, and also of love, and of reclosing ourselves in the interiority or in the intimacy of the heart, as can be observed in tantric iconography, where the *nymphaea* opens or closes in accord with places of the body and the movement of energy, of breath. We would be capable of wonder and of self-collection, both of us, as two.

The spiritual journey could, therefore, be completed between two, without the pain, the torments, the ecstasies of a solitary becoming.

Renouncing love, including carnal love, for "God", would lose its meaning since amorous relations would be transformed into weddings and festivals, both spiritual and divine. The fecundity between man and woman would not be lived primarily as a physical generation, but as a spiritual one.

Perhaps our History has developed or has been interpreted in a way which is contrary to the normal order, spiritual maternity preceding the spiritual wedding. But this wedding seems to be the highest aim of humanity, its first and last fulfillment.

It is not, therefore, in the fusion or in the ecstasy of the One that the dualism between subject and object is overcome, but rather in the incarnation of the two, a two which is irreducible to the One: man and woman. The choice is not found in duality or non-duality, but in the search of a two times one, which leaves to each person his or her unity, a unity which is limited by his or her incarnation.

The figure of two subjects who are present to each other should be added to the figure and economy of the trinitarian relationship, often present in masculine traditions, so that man and woman may find their unity.

This figure implies:

the to be in presence and alliance between two different horizons, between two subjects with a relationship of transcendence between them;

the incarnation and spiritualization of sexuate bodies;

the cultivation of sexual energy and of its verbal and gestural expressions, not merely as direct or indirect worship of a seed which is capable of generating the human species through a form of fusion.

The return to the undifferentiated in the One cannot represent the fulfillment of love's incarnation. Perhaps it represents an historical stage that is to be overcome in the movement towards a spiritual wedding between two.

Would not generating the good together represent the end of conflicts and lacerations? Wouldn't peace between us be born in the birth of the spiritual, which is neither word nor body alone, but the fruit of a love which leaves each of us to ourselves, and opens up a way for each of us to be as two?

To generate the good, to go beyond the clouds, to arrive at the sun, not merely at his light, but at him[b] as a warm, unavoidable presence, both of this world and of another. Remaining here, I have moved into the beyond with you.

For this journey, I have listened, I have opened in myself a space to accommodate you, a clearing of silence. I have welcomed this part of you, this flower of your body, born from your breath and heart, nourished by your sun, which has sprung from you and has inclined towards me. I have wanted to savor and protect this, before wanting more.

I have wanted to stop a bit. To love. Not to suffocate the breath. To allow the breath to go and to return, hotter or colder, more animated or more serene: moving air or shining cloud. I have wanted to feel you in me, not as an object, a newborn, or even as an emotion, but as life. As a living soul?

I have wanted to rise towards joy, to scale its heights, to cross the clouds, to drive back the shadows, to dispel doubt. And, moreover: to abandon what restrains, to lighten my body, to leave my arms free, floating. To dedicate myself to thought, to laugh in him, with him, in love become happiness.

Later comes the task, the work. Heavy, but light. Of different resonances, its breath fills the air, making a bridge between heaven and earth. Its range balances the profundity of silence, the absolute of solitude. The notes and tones vary unless they return to the single breath. The body becomes a musician, if it does not remain solely at the breath. In order to be incarnated, to arrive at your incarnation, it changes tones, methods. It feels, looks, listens, sings or speaks: to you, to her. Energy is made sense, inclination is made sensibility, desire becomes interiority.

But it does not agree to being separated from your body; it wants to hear your voice and, sometimes, to contemplate you. I do not want to renounce my sensible perceptions of you, those certainties which bring me consolation. Touched by you, by lights, by sounds, by forms and colors, I try to preserve this gift, without appropriating it. I receive it as a guide for my becoming, an aid for advancing along my journey.

7

To Conceive Silence

Many words have been spoken about *I Love to You*.

I find myself wondering if the work of love that the book transmits has conveyed the fact that to love each other between us, woman and man, women and men, requires the protection of a space, a place of silence.

And yet to say it in this way is not enough. I would go to the extent of saying that silence is basic for this loving relationship between the genders, a relationship which historically has yet to be thought and practiced. The origin, if I can say this, of the love between us is silence. Not so much because it rests at the level of nature, of the drives, of instinct, but because it maintains itself in difference, a difference that cannot be expressed. This silence which exists between the subjectivity of man and woman must not be overcome either in words or in representations, but must be protected, cultivated, generated, also historically, so that it becomes more refined and shared.

But not simply shared: I must protect the silence in me, and I must respect the silence of the other. Thus, silence is *two*: a two which cannot be reduced to the one or to the other, a two irreducible to one.

I will never agree with those who say that in love, including carnal love, it is possible or desirable to overcome the two. I prefer to say that a third is created, a third generated by the two but which does not belong to either. It would be a work of love different from the conception of a child, a labor of love that allows each of the two to become him/herself, in part through a recharging of energy which sometimes brings rebirth and therefore allows for becoming and perhaps even the fulfilling of a common work, while making it possible for them to remain two. This is not true for a child, which is the objectification, if I can put it this way, of the two in one and represents, in a certain sense, the death of the lovers, their alienation.

Silence, therefore, is basic to the becoming of each man and each woman and to the becoming of their relationship. Silence is at least *three*. Thanks to it, to these three, the dialectic can develop its movement. But it will not be the same as for Hegel, for whom a relationship with the masculine other and a relationship with the self are the same. Beyond the differences that exist between the two subjects: man and woman, a silence recalls that my becoming and that of the other cannot be confused. Therefore, it is never possible to overcome the other, or to overcome the relation with him in a completed or absolute objectivity.

In saying this, I have not engaged in a game of sophistry. I have not spoken solely to provoke, as I have been reproved for doing in *I Love to You*. Rather, I have heeded a lesson of the latest Western philosophers: 1) I have asked myself about the forgetfulness that seals the origin of our tradition. 2) I have taken an interest in the way of the negative. 3) I have returned to the traditions which have preceded ours, above all, to those of the Far East. 4) I have also asked myself about the separation between theology and philosophy unknown by some of those traditions.

The latest Western philosophers have already considered these points, but they have always searched for a way through a single subject and through the word, even if one can see that they were confronted with silence.

For example, what is Zarathustra doing on the mountain? What is meant by the eternal return and the word that cannot be said? What is Heidegger searching for in the poetic word and in the words of nature taught to him by his Japanese master? What is Hegel denouncing in the word of Creon? Perhaps it is the memory of a lost silence, the nostalgia for a silence to conquer.

In our tradition, silence has left itself – with disdain – to nature, to what for us is pre-given: to what is not fabricated by man and is occasionally projected onto God, except when it is entrusted to the woman in the family home. But this gesture is ambiguous: it leaves to woman the task of safeguarding the possibility of a dialectical game of love. But, in fact, man does it alone. With his techne, including his sexual techne, and his logic, he imposes upon woman a dialectic with a single subject. She can only produce children or seduce, but in a seduction that leads to nothing.

The labor of love, therefore, does not exist.

But neither is there the cultivation of a natural relationship, nor the establishment of a culture or a community which remains tied to the life and singularity of each man and each woman.

Life and singularity are erased in an abstract universal, in a familial or civil community in which this singularity is lost.

To preserve singularity in the universal becoming of subjectivity, silence must be protected, cultivated, modified, rearranged and interwoven with the word.

This culture of silence can be rediscovered[a] in two ways:

1. One is that of Buddha and the yogin and yogini. It is a cultivation of silence in relationship with nature, with one's own body and sometimes with the other, but in a master-disciple relationship ultimately to be left behind in favor of a culture of silence.

The end of this way is silence.

This can be explained in terms of a renunciation of all forms of attachment to objects which bring with them suffering caused by a requisite parcellization of the self.

Only the cultivation of the breath, of the capacity to hold the breath in oneself, corresponds to the path of self-fulfillment and happiness.

Silence, therefore, is nothing. It is not even the substantialization of itself. It is the cultivation of the relation between nature and itself, the cultivation of the relation with nature in itself.

This culture corresponds to the becoming of life thanks to the cultivation of the breath: the cultivation of inhalation, of exhalation, of restraining breath without breathing.

Again, the end of the way is silence: the reawakened, aroused practitioner speaks only through compassion. Yet this person tries to speak without losing the breath. He or she practices those modes of speaking which respect the breath: the word of praise, poetry, song are preferred to words uttered without any concern for the breath.

In Western culture, on the other hand, we – the wise – practice a mode of speaking which is logical, abstract, conceptual and a bit suffocating, which implies an almost insurmountable master-disciple relationship. The culture of the breath and of the word which respects this breath, on the other hand, procures life and autonomy. But this culture has been, for the most part, lost in our tradition.

2. There is another way to protect silence. It can, perhaps, be faithful to and interwoven with the memory of a culture of life which we have erased. This other way is found in the respect and love between man and woman, men and women, in a practice of sexual difference which exists between the two genders.

As I have already mentioned, the difference is there. It does not have to be created from nothing. We need merely be attentive to what already exists: an insuperable silence between man and woman, subjects who are irreducible to each other.

We have only, for example, to listen to the words of the girl to her mother and to those of the boy to understand that they are not the same, and that they are not to be overcome in a single discourse.

It would be useful to cultivate the difference between these words and to give each of them the possibility of being faithful to him or herself while recognizing the other. A respect of this kind, for oneself and for the other, requires a silence that our tradition has erased.

To pass to another stage of History does not mean today, and yet again, to erase everything, including the reality of a difference that is, that already exists, but rather, to interpret what is wrong in our tradition. Moreover, I would say that, in our times, we should be more concerned with refounding than with overcoming. Refounding, while keeping in mind the fact that in our tradition the word has been a means of survival – in the intellectual sense, as well – rather than a path of sharing.

Using the word for sharing requires a defense of silence which respects the life and identity of each person. Beyond the fact that I must be quiet to be attentive to the difference of the other, so that the relationship can grow, silence itself must be cultivated, for instance, in the memory of the alterity of the other-man and in the memory of myself as woman.

Silence remains two, and perhaps even three, in the construction of a history: the future must stay partly silent so that the other can construct it together with me. This silence is (these silences are) the guarantor(s) that conflict cannot push itself as far as the death of either one of us. It guarantees that conflict, if there is any, will be limited and that it will be more about playing than killing, about helping to give birth or to remain in oneself than about giving death.

Silence, which is the guardian of nature, of life, of difference, prevents these conflicts of the same which lead to death, conflicts about which Hegel speaks (as well as Jean-Paul Sartre and Maurice Merleau-Ponty). We have only to remember the master-slave dialectic or the fact that, for Hegel, wars are necessary to move from one period of History to another.

If the construction of History were to be made by two, these struggles for life or death, these wars between the past and the future would no longer be necessary: the two would no longer have to be overcome in the one. The limit of irreducibility would safeguard the singularity of each person: "you who are not and will never be me or mine" would remain you as I would remain me, thanks to the work of the negative, which entails respect for our difference.

But how is this to be accomplished at the level of community? Before being accused of utopian idealism, I will respond that silence is a better guarantor of reality than is the concept,[b] and that it better protects a non-idealistic becoming.

I will then say that to permit the possibility of this silence *to* and *of* each person, it is necessary that the identity of each be guaranteed by a personal right: for example, by a civil code for real persons which leaves to each word and silence.

This space of articulation between word and silence for each man and each woman requires that both the State and the family lose their authority over the word and over silence.

The "marriage contract" would then become a contract between two different civil persons who preserve their identity rather than losing it in the unity of the familial institution.

The State would become a servant or administrator at the service of citizens. It would never be their master, their lord, he who imposes on them his law, his word.

What we are talking about, then, is a new relationship between two, as well as a new communitarian relation, both of which are necessary to continue the construction of History.

I Love to You was thought and written to remember the encounter between two people, to continue the construction of their history, and of History itself, in view of a greater happiness. This work is based on the recognition of sexual difference, of the irreducibility between man and woman, men and women; an irreducibility which should be treated as a civil and cultural value, and not only as a natural reality to be overcome in culture and in community.

8

Between us, a fabricated world

There is much that is strange,[a] but nothing
that surpasses man in strangeness.[b]
He sets sail on the frothing waters
amid the south winds of winter
tacking through the mountains
and furious chasms of the waves.
He wearies even the noblest
of the gods, the Earth,
indestructible and untiring,
overturning her from year to year,
driving the plows this way and that
with horses.

And man, pondering and plotting,
snares the light-gliding birds
and hunts the birds of the wilderness
and the native creatures of the sea.
With guile he overpowers the beast
that roams the mountains by day as by night,
he yokes the hirsute neck of the stallion
and the undaunted bull.

And he has found his way
to the resonance of the word,
and to wind-swift-understanding,
and to the courage of rule over cities.
He has considered also how to flee
from exposure to the arrows
of unpropitious weather and frost.

Everywhere journeying, inexperienced and without issue,
he comes to nothingness.
Through no flight can he resist

the one assault of death,
even if he has succeeded in cleverly evading
painful sickness.

Clever indeed, mastering
the ways of skill beyond all hope,
he sometimes accomplishes evil,
sometimes achieves his brave deeds.

He wends his way between the laws of the earth
and the adjured justice of the gods.
Rising high above his place,
he who for the sake of adventure takes
the nonessent for essent loses
his place in the end.

May such a man never frequent my hearth;
May my mind never share the presumption
of him who does this.

Sophocles, Antigone (lines 332–75)[1]

The sea is frightening, but man is more terrible still.

Man leaves solid ground, the soil, his dwelling, the reassuringly familiar, to venture out into the sea – not a calm sea, but a tempestuous one, a bottomless abyss. This abyss remains exterior to him, foreign to the abyss of interiority. Recognizing the irreducible difference of the other opens an abyss in consciousness, in knowledge, in truth. It seems that man chooses to ignore this irreducible difference, preferring instead to perceive and project this abyss onto the cosmic. But it is onto the sea that he first projects it.

Yet in addition to the violence which he imposes upon the sea, man exerts another kind of violence upon the earth, the great goddess.

Man upsets the rhythm of natural growth. He plows the earth and obliges it to produce by force what it does not yield on its own: he accelerates the time of production, imports seeds from afar.

Man imposes a yoke upon the life that unfolds in itself but whose foundation he does not inhabit.

Is this not because he feels foreign to this life which lives without him, this life which reproduces itself, which orders itself without his governance?

Is this not a possible reason for the beginning of History? Is History not simply the other name for man's intolerance towards nature?

From then on, does History not move in an opposite direction: towards the oblivion of man's to be?

The most violent gesture related to this oblivion is, "at the beginning", a gesture of mastery by means of which man wants to substitute his power for nature's strength.

The unfolding of the beginning occurs later and is weakened through its generalization. At the same time, it becomes insignificant and excessive. It grows in quantity and number, but not in magnitude and strength.

The uncanny is the gesture of initial dominion which will always force man to tame things, in particular, those things which he produces.

The beginning of History cannot reveal itself in primordial bones or in the unearthing of primitive artefacts. Rather, this beginning is revealed in the interpretation of a mythology in which man imposes himself as the master of nature, after having been its slave. Initially, man's mastery resembles the natural strength with which he wishes to measure himself: that of the sea, of wild animals.

His gesture of dominion and the instruments which serve this domination: tools, language, intellect, the passions themselves, create, little by little, another world which dominates him – in the form of History, for example – and which exiles him from himself, even if he may feel closer to it because it is made by him.

Man thus appears surrounded by a double power: the power of the universe around him and that of the world created by him which he does not recognize as his work, in particular as the work of his violence which is concealed in the everyday.

Man lives in the uncanny, believing that he has tamed it. For him, the familiar is his violence become History. But in such a place, generated by his dominion, he is an exile.

Man has become estranged from his to be and thinks in an improper fashion. He considers himself to be the master of the very thing which dominates him.

He believes himself to be the creator of language, of poetry, of reason, but, in fact, he has only imitated the strength of the universe which surrounds him. He is nothing but an effect of the violence which results from his conquest.

He has not discovered what he is by contemplating nature, the flowers, and others, but by taming, plowing up, and capturing.

Such would be the self-same of Western man: the effect of a mastery, of a violent dominion over the natural universe and not of a respect for, a contemplation of, a praise for or an alliance with it.

But in wanting to act like the universe in its most violent aspect, and not with it in its beauty and wisdom, man has forgotten this world, has forgotten himself.

The fact that his impulses, inclinations, and desires are violent does not necessarily mean that this is an inherent part of the masculine to be, but that violence can come from an historical construction.

This pushes Kant, without his knowledge, to discover his model of the sublime in the tempest, and not in the tranquil rising of the sun. Perhaps the stormy sea reminds him of something which is key to his journey as historical man. In the tempest, Kant finds what is most uncanny and most violent about the beginning of his history; a trace of the foundation of his identity is revealed to him therein. He calls the surfacing of this memory sublime: not terrible or horrible, but sublime because he does not master it.

It says much about the interpretation of our rationality that Kant has been led to a complete reawakening(?) by what is most uncanny rather than, for example, by a cultivation of the perceptions.

We are very far away indeed from a figure like Buddha, for whom reawakening takes place beginning from the contemplation of the most simple, of the most everyday, of the least extraordinary and violent: the contemplation of a flower. Such a gesture cannot be weakened nor can its profundity be lost by extension: contemplating ten flowers is no better than contemplating one; quite to the contrary. The perfection of the act is achieved through a cultivation of the senses. In the unfolding of a history, it is not the number of gestures which determines the fulfillment of contemplation. Rather, contemplation occurs in the encounter between two cultivated natures: between a flower as a production of the earth's beauty and the gaze of Buddha as the place where its body flowers, both of which are open thanks to the light of the sun, micro- and macrocosmic.

Such contemplation joins the in-itself and the outside-of-itself in a single relationship which does not require a new construction: it is matter and form together. It is perfect in itself and does not deform itself by becoming too big, sublime, monstrous, and thus imperceptible to the gaze, to the senses.

In our culture, the passage to the universal often represents a loss of understanding of the sensible and of truth, due to their generalization. From then on, women are the guardians of singularity, of a sensible understanding which is opposed to abstract extension. Unfortunately, their qualities are still considered as being bound only to nature, to matter, a situation which carries with it the risk of again falling away from the intellect and into immediate sensibility.

But an interpretation of this sort signifies oblivion, a lack of thought. The properties of feminine identity remain yet to be thought, not beginning from the violent actions of the masculine, but through a cultivation of the to be woman which may even be capable of redirecting man to his own to be.

The feminine is not called to carry out the task of constructing a world which is similar to man's: a violent, uncanny world, which exists through the domination of nature, of animals, of other humans.

To become a world herself, to cultivate herself without violence or power over what surrounds her – all of these correspond more to the feminine to be.

Mastering oneself without sacrifice, amputation, or self-annulment opens up the horizon of a new culture about which the Far East has left us certain elements to remember and to meditate upon. Here, human becoming unfolds in a way which is different from the becoming of Western man, who "with violence leaves his dwelling and plows up, captures, tames".[c]

Following the example set by the Far East, culture would correspond to self-mastery rather than to going outside of the self in order to dominate others and to impose upon them an order which is perhaps less harmonious than the natural, primitive one.

In reality, the tempest belongs to an ensemble composed not of violence but of harmony. Nonetheless, Western man chooses to measure himself against the terrible rather than the calm. He remembers the frightening aspect of nature and forgets its mild sweetness. He likes to tame the infuriated sea, the wild animals, the unbridled passions. He restrains with force the violence of what surrounds him, a violence which only he can domesticate.

The natural environment becomes wild, the perceived adversary against whom he must fight. All that exists is reduced to what man must overcome. Beginning from his entry, he recreates it in order to dominate it. From this intention results the universe as violence.

From then on, what exists, what is, has lost a sensible relationship with man, and has also lost a way of exchange through the word.

The being sea, the being earth, living beings are named by him only after having been yoked by him, only after he has interrupted all proximity and reciprocity with them, as well as all attentiveness to them.

Does not, perhaps, the key to or the beginning of the world's mystery lie in man's desire to keep the center of the whole in himself? He does not want to share it or to recognize that the universe moves starting from its own center, independently of him.

Man could have envisioned it as his task to contemplate the intimate harmony of the world's motion, admitting that its origin remains unknown to him. But he cannot endure the mystery of the other and, instead, conceives a god made in his own image in order to encircle, if not to dominate, the horizon of every mystery.

Man represents a center only on the condition that he respects the center of the other, that he recognizes the center of the natural universe and that of every living creature, especially of every human creature.

The history constructed by man resembles a history of enduring violence, of appropriation, of domination, and not of a contribution to what is. Man has created, invented, and given to nature not so much because he was more than her, but because he wished to tame her. Is this not, perhaps, because he was less than her?

Only if we understand that the use of power in language, in understanding, in forming and building helps to create (i.e.

always, to bring forth) the violent act of laying out paths into the
environing power of the essent, only then shall we understand
the strangeness, the uncanniness of all violence. For man, as he
journeys everywhere, is not without issue in the external sense
that he comes up against outward barriers and cannot go on. In
one way or another he can always go farther into the etcetera.
He is without issue because he is always thrown back on the
paths that he himself has laid out: he becomes mired in his paths,
caught in the beaten track, and thus caught he compresses the
circle of his world, entangles himself in appearance, and so
excludes himself from being. He turns round and round in his
own circle. He can ward off whatever threatens this limited
sphere. He can employ every skill in its place. The violence that
originally creates the paths engenders its own mischief of versa-
tility, which is intrinsically issueless, so much so that it bars itself
from reflection about the appearance in which it moves. All
violence shatters against *one* thing. That is death.[2d]

But in opening a passage for himself, man becomes mired, loses
himself between the real and what he has fabricated, and in short,
loses the way of his to be. He turns round and round within his
own circle, the circle of his dominion. He makes everything that
enters into the circle his own, subjecting it to his perspective,
increasingly forgetting the path of what is, and of who is. He loses
himself in the appearance of those things imagined or made by
him, which he calls the world. This becomes, for him, a type of
second nature ignorant of naturalness or of the natural.

Paths thus traced produce disorder and inconstancy, uncertainty,
doubt. One thing and one thing only prevails over the violence of
man: death. Is this not, perhaps, because it is absolute violence?
Death can be neither tamed nor deciphered, in spite of the
knowledge of science. It is not a fact or an event amongst others:
man defines himself through a relationship with death. The to be
of man is constituted thanks to the limit of death: he has nothing
which can overcome it.

The fact remains that man places himself here on earth in a
circle woven of violence and dismay, thus closing every opening.

Man reaches a point where he dismays even himself, because
his violent to be has made him misplace every relationship with
the familiar.

Violence, the violent result from machinations carried out through techne. It is this way in the fabrication of ships which tame the sea and of plows which force the earth to produce beyond its natural fertility. It is the same for knowledge, understood not in the sense of gaining consciousness or a cognizance of what exists, of that which presents itself to man, but in the sense of a knowledge which goes beyond what exists. For Western man, culture develops as a desire to remove from his mystery the to be which is originally foreign to him. It develops as a desire to measure himself against this secret until it reveals itself, until it becomes an appearance. For example, according to man, the earth's fertility remains a sealed mystery and cultivating it signifies, in a certain sense, forcing the mystery to appear. But this involves violating and fragmenting the fertility of the earth into various types of technical knowledge which unveil, at least partially, the mystery.

The same thing happens to us: sociology, psychology, ethnology attempt to unveil the mystery of the to be which we are. But these sciences parcel us out to different kinds of knowledge, transforming our to be into different types of apparent beings. In so doing, they distance us from our to be, turning us inside out, exhausting the reserves of our to be, emptying us of our capacity to be, dragging us to our own oblivion.

Everything which can be enumerated from the outside – thanks to the different sciences – about man on the one hand and woman on the other, cannot uncover a great deal either about man's or woman's to be. Such knowledge wants to unveil the mystery of the to be which we are, but the violence of their method annihilates it.

The to be is constituted beginning from a center of interiority which integrates, at different levels of profundity, the multiple dimensions of our existence: corporeal, psychic, genealogical, sociological ... When described from without, these integrations become nothing: they have meaning in so far as they compose and organize a whole, constituting us in a unity, an identity made of subjectivity and objectivity. Man's relationship with techne has led us to believe that the human can be understood from without. As Heidegger writes, a knowledge of this type assumes the use of a means turned to an end and to an activity on man's behalf.

*

When he said "man", Heidegger was not thinking of the masculine gender, or at least he did not designate it as such. Is it not perhaps true that techne, the mystery of the reign of techne, can be explained beginning from a masculine subjectivity which is unaware of itself?

Various reasons lead man to privilege techne: a manufacturing outside of himself, a placing in front of himself, an external unveiling, a manifesting of truth in an other with force and skill.

This is probably related to man's relationship with the one who generates him: he will never generate in himself and must fabricate things outside of himself, in order to separate himself from the mother; he must manufacture externally, while she generates internally.

Man generates and loves outside of himself, even when he fabricates and cultivates outside of himself in order to exist, in order to be. This way of producing is his alone. Woman becomes or allows becoming in herself: whether of herself or of the other. She allows all becoming in herself: of woman, of child, of man. If she does not produce (like) man, if she does not go outside of herself and reduce herself to nothing, woman becomes herself in herself.

Doubtless, she can still remain an instrument for man's technical production. Thus, the prostitute is utilized for playing with body-nature in spite of the mother, the wife is used to bear children, to take care of the house, to look after the matter with which man can continue to produce, fabricate, and become.

The to be of Western man is individuated – even in philosophy and religion – beginning from a technical knowledge which privileges exteriority. This reality is clearly found in our age of techne.

Technical knowledge does not only appear in the form of nuclear centers or artificial insemination. It is true to say, however, that it always takes the path of fabrication, the fabrication of a material or spiritual thing to which man, with the intention of using it to achieve his own ends, gives a form. In this way, man has created, bit by bit, a world which he places between him and himself, between himself and the feminine world.[c]

9

She before the king

As our culture has unfolded, it has moved from concrete singularity and towards abstract universality.

In Sophoclean tragedy, the figure of Antigone incarnates a concrete singularity and its ties with a concrete collectivity. The chorus also participates in this singularity.

In this way, Antigone and, to some extent the chorus, remember the difference between day and night, the difference between the seasons. They remember the earth and the gods of the home, they remember those who are near, in the first place the family, but also the citizens and ancestors of the city.

This reveals itself in the actions of Antigone, and also in her words about the citizens and ancestors of the kingdom of Thebes.

Antigone's discourse is simple, always with content and poetic style.

Antigone never expresses herself in a solely abstract manner, never debates or quarrels with arguments that are unrelated to a present message. Her reasoning does not unfold on the level of simple understanding.

The style of the chorus is more abstract, oscillating between two existing discourses in the tragedy. In general, the chorus approaches Antigone's manner of speaking, but it is also an arbiter which is no longer free: it represents the effects of a fear of the tyrant. Antigone, faithful to herself, always preserves her own style.

For Antigone, attention to the other comes before retreat into blind egoism. She affirms that, without this care for the other, life is not worth living. For her, to live means to respect love, the laws of nature and those of the city: the home, the family, those close to her. Her law – neither simply civil nor simply religious – is not abstract or empty. It does not deal solely with the ownership of goods, but concerns respect for persons, for concrete persons, for persons who surround us: neighbors, those closest to us.

Creon's discourse manifests:

simple egoism: immediate or calculated;

arbitrary power founded upon a bestowed command and the
obligation to obey: for example, the prohibition against burying
Polyneices;

the use of force to impose order: armed force, the right to kill;

the passage from singularity to abstract universality in order to
establish such a power.

Thus, Creon sacrifices those who are closest to him – his family,
his people – to an abstract or tyrannical dominion, a dominion
founded upon nothing if not the means of legitimating the
government of a single man.

The means employed are: terror, the right to put to death, scorn
for the gods of the hearth, the abandonment of natural laws –
both cosmic and familial – and of the popular sentiments tied to
place and to traditions.

Creon builds his kingdom on an empty space with an abstract
logic, with the use of force and terror, with the self-conferral of a
right which will be law for others, and with a government based
upon a formal order which is arbitrary and lacking content. He
thinks that he can substitute a power made possible by artifice for
a respect for traditions, for the earth, and for the citizens.

Creon's manner of speaking is poor, without poetry, while at
the same time rational and hypersubjective. Even if he begins by
arguing with logic, he cannot sustain his argument with rigor.

His egological power rests on the fact that he is a man, that he
is a father, that he is a king, depending upon the person to whom
he turns. It is not founded upon the content of a message, upon a
truth proper to an identity, or upon a political program.

Upon woman, Creon imposes himself as man, upon the son as
father, upon the people as leader, upon the soothsayer as truth itself.

The content of his discourse amounts to an abstract affirmation
of himself, to the fear of his own loss, to the terror he inflicts, and
to various arguments devoid of any reasoning based in reality.

Creon abandons the reality and the truth of the in-itself (if I
can speak in an anachronistic manner . . .) for an authoritarian,

formal and abstract for-itself. His skill and audacity are not based on just any reality: they are a challenge to what is, they establish their power from the simple opposition to what exists.

Creon represents the passage to what is fabricated: to what distances itself from real existence or being in order to exercise itself as simple human ability. To this extent, he is on the earth and outside of the earth, he is in the city and outside of the city, he is a father but he is estranged from kinship, he is a man but he is estranged from masculine identity, he is the King of Thebes but he is estranged from kingship.

He resembles a simple, abstract consciousness. His audacity exceeds what is, rises beyond itself and does not know a return to itself, in itself. What Creon affirms does not correspond to what is. To be man means only to oppose himself to woman, or to subjugate her. It does not involve conforming to a to be, to an appearance, to a becoming, to a duty, to what is in reality. It is a proclamation which attempts to impose itself, to define itself through the exercise of a power, and not through the constitution of a concrete identity.

In response to the question: who is Creon?, the answer could be: he is nothing, he is only the challenge coming from an ability that wants to dominate. He is an "I" without content, a mirage-like "I" which confuses itself with an arbitrary authority, an "I" which defines itself as a he/it or an He/It[a] to be respected in the name of an artificial necessity.

Must the exercise of government correspond to an "I" without content? My answer is: no. The pure exercise of power, pure representation, cannot exist. This is not so for Creon: he is not elected, he is king by virtue of blood, but he imposes an artificial domination which is fabricated and egoistical. In the radicalness of such a change of rule, perhaps Creon demonstrates that the exercise of government by a single gender is always tyrannical.

Could Creon be elected by everyone? The discourses of men and women are so different that it is difficult to imagine that there could only be one same elected official for the two genders. In which language will this person speak, whether man or woman?

At a formal level, the question arises as to how the community's representative will be named. For example: will we say legislator[b] or legislatress[c] in the case of an elected woman? For a woman, does not accepting to be legislator signify choosing a power which resembles that of Creon: an abstract power, not based on a natural or real identity? With such a point of departure, the representation no longer conforms to what exists.

Certainly I am not about to defend a kingdom founded on the family, a royal or aristocratic power based on natural heredity, on ties of blood. I will not say that such a rule is good in itself, but neither will I say that it is enough to be an elected official – estranged from bloodties and natural genealogy – in order to exercise a just government. We know today that a democratically elected head of government can be equally as tyrannical as a king. His barbarity can be even worse because his power is in a certain sense fabricated, more arbitrary and, to this extent, in even greater error.

As the chorus says, what is made by man's hand sometimes tends towards the good, sometimes towards the bad. Fabrication does not have in itself a good end, and the culture based on it is not in itself good. Thus, man finds it necessary to create gods of the beyond to manage his world.

However, such a gesture often drags man into a state where he forgets his relationships with others, even when he is being pushed by an intention to create his own universe.

Fabrication is not good in itself, and an entire period of History is often necessary to allow us to see its outcome. This is not the case for a living organism: a human body or nature itself. As the chorus says in Sophocles' tragedy, man's ability does not necessarily imply in itself a good or an assured future. Once again, the earth demonstrates if the gesture is good or bad, appropriate or not. And the same holds true for the body of the living.

But the fabricated world, the fabricated human are no longer in a position to distinguish between the just and the unjust, the fair and the unfair, the good and the bad. And not even we, in so far as we are already artificial individuals, reduced to the impersonality of a "one", to any transcendence whatsoever[d] – as Sartre would say – can do it any longer. It is up to us to rediscover a measure, certain valid measures.

The chorus proclaims: a measure belongs to the earth, that most sublime divinity, which enjoys a statute and laws. A measure exists for the earth, understood as the cosmic universe: with its sun, its seas, its mountains, its own space-time, its birds, its fish, its wild animals.

Man's skill cannot transgress this measure, otherwise the earth reacts. She does not avenge herself, as we could imagine, we who are fabricated humans and made nervous by our productions. In the earth, disorder is produced: she loses her measure, her harmony, her beauty, her fecundity.

Another measure corresponds to the relations between humans. Its task is complex in so much as it must ensure and harmonize several diverse types of relationships: those between nature and culture, those between ties of kinship, those which concern genealogy and alliance.

These last are in a certain way tied to government. At first, they ensured to government those relations that generate and repair life: earth and woman, lover and mother. Governing, therefore, involved a measure for life, a measure for the relationships between the living, and a measure for community based on natural necessities: food, love, reproduction. Humans united for the purpose of searching out and exchanging the nutriment necessary for life. They united to secure more or less natural shelters, gather food and fulfill all of the other requirements of love, including those dictated by the needs of their children.

Love was the legislator:ᶜ a love neither voluntary nor obligated, but one of peaceful coexistence, one of common sense and of the measure necessary for life. Various feminine figures have represented it: Aphrodite, Demeter, Anne and Mary.

At a later point, the father imposed himself as the sole lord and master, and even man. But this power takes little account of natural necessities: it is in large part arbitrary and fabricated. By imposing upon nature an inappropriate order, this power ruins it. The human being, enslaved to drives and passions, loses the measure of himself as a whole individual in relationship with nature, the other, others. From this moment, the relationship with the natural returns to what Hegel calls natural immediacy, but this immediacy is already outside of a natural harmony. History loses the measure adapted to nature and unfolds according to a fabricated order. The relationship with nature encloses itself within the family, within the home, where natural immediacy is allowed, on the condition that children are conceived and that a work force is produced, and, for the woman, on the condition that she submit herself to her husband's desire.

The relation with the natural is refolded into the family, into the home, but these are under the dominion of the father – who is their head – and they are also at the service of the State. But of the relationship between woman and man, in particular the possible exploitation between them, the State does not want to know anything. It is a private matter, as they say. The State's interest in the family is confined to the production of children and a labor force ... The tie between those in the home is removed from law. The civil community prefers to ignore the way in which woman's relationship with herself and man's with himself is accomplished in the familial sphere. Instead, it indirectly encourages the exploitation of nature, closing its eyes to the sexual violence exhibited today in the city, and sometimes "paying" for the birth of one more child.

As Hegel writes, woman and man lose their identity in the family. The labor of love does not return as a for-itself for either one: it becomes children, the ownership of goods.

Hegel adds that the love between man and woman remains in a state of natural immediacy and is not capable, as such, of assuring the passage to culture, even if, in a certain sense, it is more just than a simply fabricated power. Or rather, the relationship with nature is more just because a measure exists in it: a respect for and cultivation of what lives. But this more just relationship Hegel situates between brother and sister, where the blood relationship is, according to him, in balance, while it would be out of balance in the relationship between man and woman. Why would the relationship between brother and sister represent an equilibrium? It could be more impassioned, to the extent that neither of them has a proper identity, tied as they are through blood to their parents, in particular to the mother.

But what by now we experience as natural immediacy is sometimes already distant from the natural. We have become fabricated humans. In order to reach something natural, we speak of the fact:

1) that the love between woman (women) and man (men) is "natural";

2) that reproduction is obligatory: it, therefore, is no longer an ornament of love, but a duty imposed by the State or by the Church in the name of nature.

What nature leaves us is the instinct to violence – even though we consider ourselves human because we have tamed wild animals – and the obligation to reproduce: two perversions of our being human.

The rigor of Hegel can teach us that a third way is missing: a culture which corresponds to the objectivity of our destiny as sexuate beings. For this culture, there needs to be two subjects of different genders, not subjugated to the ties of blood. In this way, the natural can become culture without anything being missing from ethicality. This is the stage which Hegel could not realize either as a past history of the becoming of the spirit or as an opening to a possible future.

Hegel does not imagine that the relationship between woman and man can be a tie of culture. According to him, it remains uncultivated "natural immediacy" which the ethico-genealogical order tempers.

But such an order appears tied to a naturality that opposes itself to the universal becoming of the spirit, with man as the mediator between the two orders. The family remains a substantial, undifferentiated unity. The relationship of sensibility and of love between man and woman is not its foundation: each shares the ethical task of alienating him or herself in familial unity and, in this way, of being at the service of the State. Structurally, the family appears to be based upon the imperatives imposed by religion and by the State rather than upon an alliance between man and woman. They are united in God or in the State to ensure the survival of human nature. Their ethical task corresponds to ancestor worship, to respecting the "*patria*" to which they must pay their taxes, to guaranteeing food for their spouses and children, to reproducing.

Spiritualizing nature, in particular through carnal desire, does not seem to be a work entrusted to the man and woman who wed: they remain, as bodies, tied to an uncultivated nature, subjected to a State and to a religion in complicity with each other.

Perhaps such a religion has not discovered its way, its method for spiritualizing the natural world. It remains a religion split between nature and culture, a religion that has not completed the transmutation of sexual desire into a proper interiority which, at the same time, does not annul this desire.

Philosophers like Hegel and Heidegger have thought that a living being's in-gathering is not possible outside of the horizon of death. A member of a family, for example, can experience himself as whole only by comparing himself to death. Thus, one sees that familial sentiment is, above all, based on the veneration of the dead. These philosophers could not have imagined that, within the sphere of a culture in which the subject remains one, belonging to a gender could represent a limit capable of protecting life while remaining internal to it. The difference between feminine and masculine identity, there thanks to the negativity tied to a respect for one's own gender, opens up the possibility of a new alliance between them.

This type of loving relationship between the sexes would not reduce itself to the instinctual, to what remains in part desire, nor would it limit itself to natural immediacy. It absolutely would not forget sensibility: it would emerge as the love of each for the other, made possible thanks to a difference which opens a subjective exchange in which the word intervenes.

An alliance of this sort between man and woman allows them to leave the natural unity of the family and to escape the exclusive power of genealogy.

Such an alliance still remains unthought in our tradition because the subject, consciousness, are always conceived as *one*: one and multiple, but not two, two which are different, two which are irreducible.

In the sphere of a double subjectivity, man and woman communicate, but not in a language which has been codified and which neutralizes the two. They speak to each other beginning from their mutual necessity; for example, from their carnal and spiritual love.

The alliance between man and woman becomes, therefore, a bridge between nature and culture, a bridge which has yet to be built.

10

Each transcendent to the other

Today, our desperation and impotence often express themselves in the form of slogans. We proclaim that we want to be free, equal, brothers. But we do so without considering the meaning that these words have in the context of our era and without thinking about the conditions in which liberty, equality, and fraternity are practicable.

In our fabricated world, we can proclaim our demands. But I doubt that the walls of the subway or the noise of machines are changed as a result. We shout, but who listens to us? A variety of worlds separates us: the world of techne, the world of calculation, the world of science, the world of culture. We almost never face each other. We think that we encounter each other but, most of the time, we are infinitely distant. Separated by the infinite, to be precise. I will attempt to explain this in regard to freedom.

Roughly two hundred years ago, in an era in which philosophers took the time to think, and to think about what man is, whether alone or in community, and about what he could become, some of them discussed the nature of freedom.

I will try to relay the meaning of their discussions and uncertainties. They are still topical, and a philosophy of sexual difference can contribute to resolving some of their aporias.

Certainly, these philosophers did not believe that it was enough to shout "I want to be free" in order to be so. Nor did they think that it was enough to locate the oppression or oppressor outside of themselves and to believe that, if I am not free, it is only because of an other, others, or a thing outside of me: a master, for example. Rather, they considered the problem of how to be free in themselves, placing it in terms of their own subjectivity, in terms of their own consciousness. They asked themselves: what can freedom be for me, a human subject?

Since they had not lost their reason completely, they knew at least this: it is not enough to shout "I want to be free" one more time to become so. And they often said that freedom is always defined with reference to non-freedom, to an obstacle or to an impediment, to a self-alienation. But obstacles, impediments, and alienation are not simply external. They are also within me.

Therefore, they asked, how do I overcome that which in me, in us, prevents freedom? They had not yet posed the question of the between-us, at least in the sense in which I am attempting to think it and in the way in which it is beginning to be posed in our time. Instead, each one asked himself about his freedom, about the freedom of his consciousness, as if it were the universal model of every human consciousness. Thus, each was concerned with finding, at the same time, the right solution for himself and for everyone.

But all of these philosophers were men and they were debating between men. Their solution was, of course, a masculine one.

They posed the question in these terms: we live between subjectivity and objectivity; but an objectivity outside of me must not impose its law upon me, or I am no longer free. For example, God must not be a God-Object outside of me, foreign to the becoming of my subjectivity. Rather, God must be the one who contributes to the becoming of this subjectivity, having already been established by me, or in me, as the blind font of my consciousness, of my project, of my becoming, of my horizon.

I have used the example of God as the exteriority which cannot alienate my freedom because these philosophers need God but, at the same time, do not want to be blinded, alienated, rendered unconscious or unfree by Him.[a]

They need God as an external limit to their subjectivity, to their horizon, to their project. They also need God as a place which determines their subjectivity as objectivity. Only God would be capable of objectively defining who I am. Moreover, my intention needs an end in order to go-towards, and God would be the objective situated at the infinity of my intention. Being at the infinite, God alone would see me as an objectivity, and it is for this reason that God is necessary for me. Indeed, subjectivity needs an objective frame within which to constitute itself, and subjectivities need objective references to link themselves to each other, otherwise each exceeds the limits of the other.

For these philosophers, therefore, God is necessary but not alienating. If God is necessary as the condition for an objective point of view relating to my subjectivity, he is still more so as a pole which has, in some ways, been overturned by my natural instincts and inclinations. Here is, in fact, the other pole which obstructs my freedom: my natural inclinations, my passions, my immediate sensibility. The objectivity which alienates my inner freedom is, thus, two-fold: 1) my human nature, my instincts in particular; 2) God, if He remains an objectivity outside of me.

How does one navigate between these two extremes?, these philosophers asked themselves, either consciously or unconsciously. And as players in a game of chess, they placed God both within their game and outside of it, but still as the very condition of it.

Kant said: God must remain a hypothesis outside of my consciousness who, however, allows me freely to give meaning to my decisions. As a consequence, God is a sort of ultimate foundation, an imaginary fire which allows me to give meaning to my consciousness, since He represents an infinite understanding in that finitude which is mine. For other philosophers, Fichte and also Maimonides, the infinite is contained in me if I am finite. The infinite is not a hypothesis or a point of view which I give myself in order to think but is, instead, a reality in me. God and the divine are imagined as essents in me because they are necessary for me: for example, as a font or resource of tension towards an infinite horizon, as union, even, between intuition and understanding.

For these male philosophers, God corresponds to an indispensable creation, to a human necessity. According to them, God is necessary for freedom, for thought.

This God is used to overcome nature and, in this manner, protects my freedom. He does not have to be objective. He cannot be confused with a determinate objectivity, with an object outside of me, which can alienate me. Instead, He is the name of what allows me to become, to define meaning, the meaning, to overcome my instincts, etc.

God is necessary, according to these philosophers, for the domination of nature, of my nature. Thanks to Him, I determine how to overcome my inclinations, with a force that is contrary to them and which safeguards my freedom.

I progress, distancing myself from myself, in particular from my nature, from nature.

For these solitary philosophers, for these philosophies based upon a single subject who is, moreover, masculine, the problem is always:

giving oneself subjectivity despite a natural birth, that is in spite of being born and not created;
defining oneself as a subject in opposition to nature and against the self in so far as it is natural;
defining oneself against mother-nature thanks to a totally-Other – God, Father – towards whom, by means of whom, beginning from whom, I become: freedom, culture, spirit, desire, love, word, intelligence, reason, etc . . .

The subject develops between these two extremes: nature and God, nature and spirit, mother-nature and father, irreducible birth and absolute creation. The subject is free to move from a like beginning to a like end. Such is the meaning of freedom: to lift oneself above nature with the help of a God who is "hidden", necessary but hidden.

We will suspend, for the moment, the question of knowing who or what God is. If we return, instead, to the becoming of the subject, we see that our philosophers encounter another difficulty. In order to pass from nature to freedom, the subject must, according to them, take on an active becoming against the inclinations of nature, in some ways against his own sensibility. But since they are intelligent, these sages understand that it is not possible to maintain subjectivity without sensibility. And, by the definition of their subjective journey, their sensibility is not easy to protect or to define, except perhaps in aesthetics or in art, the place of which, however, is not so easy to establish between nature and culture, mother and father, body and spirit, natural inclinations and freedom, art and reproduction, or as a creation of nature.

Let us also leave art aside for the moment, to ask ourselves how these philosophers, wishing to achieve the absolute of culture, the universal of consciousness, can protect their sensibility.

The solution is roughly the same as the one that is found in the opposition nature/spirit, natural inclinations/freedom. It is now a matter of resorting to another absolute, at which the subject will never arrive, and which, because it exists, leaves him passively sensible: whether the unfabricated thing in itself or the transcendental object.

The transcendental object is that towards which the subject aims but which he will never possess. It corresponds to a frame, an intention, an obstacle which allows him to progress: from nature to spirit, from empiria to a thought which is not empirical, at least immediately. This transcendental object, because it is unattainable, returns the subject to passive sensibility: the subject is involved by the transcendental object, but he cannot involve it. The transcendental object, like God, appears as a construction, a creation, an invention – neither visible nor perceptible – of the philosophical subject, necessary for the completion of his own journey.

If all of this seems subtle, coherent and intelligible, it nevertheless depends upon certain *a prioris*:

the subject is one, and always the same;

nature, my nature, is evil; the spirit, instead, is good;

every subject is placed under the same laws;

a universal exists which is true for everyone.

I will present a few objections to the type of subjective journey proposed by such philosophers which, at least for those who are still alive, will perhaps give an indication of how to resolve the existing contradictions, oppositions, and difficulties.

1. It seems to me that not only nature, but also culture, can obstruct our freedom.

It has become evident today that the fabricated character of culture itself can alienate us.

It is clear with respect to techne and the world that it imposes upon us with its external laws (see Sartre's analysis of the manufactured object as that which transforms us into just any transcendental[b]).

It is not yet as clear, however, when it comes to thinking of culture as language, religion, philosophy, art, etc ... We are not yet aware enough of the fact that man's spiritual becoming does not resemble woman's. Nor are we fully aware of the fact that the culture of one era of History does not necessarily apply to another, that it is not necessarily universal, and that this deserves a bit of reflection: which, however, does not mean destroying the entire tradition.

It is not even sufficiently clear that constituting the subject on the basis of his relationship with an object could be a form of alienation.

In short, what still remains hidden is the limit of a culture based upon a single subject. We fail to see that this culture impedes intersubjectivity, particularly between the two genders, defining, for example, objectivity and all the forms of representation according to a single subject, thus alienating them from the other gender, and from a relationship between two.

In other words, what must be surmounted for the becoming of our freedom is not only a natural pre-given but also a cultural one. We are born in a culture in which it is not always clear what belongs to our nature and what belongs to a culture foreign to it. We must, therefore, interpret our culture as a determination which can possibly alienate our becoming.

2. In order to overcome this alienation, we must rethink our relationship with nature, especially since masculine philosophy has always considered objectivity as a constructed reality, at times through auto-reflection, and never as a given. As a result, masculine culture has generally ignored the objectivity which exists in the pre-given: the body, bodies, the cosmic universe. Perhaps it is no longer necessary, as has been taught, that we be ordered, that we be allowed to accede to subjectivity by a foreign language which, to a certain degree, parallels our nature, our body. Our body itself carries those measures which lead to a respect for each person and for the relationship between.

Indeed, the universe – micro- or macrocosmic – obeys certain laws before any sort of work of man[c] or any sort of creation of God[d]: their intervention does not have meaning except when it recognizes this original order.

I would thus raise an objection to our philosophers' discussion of a limit to freedom which does not consider the laws of the body and of the cosmic world.

I would ask them why they seek objectivity only outside of the self, when it can already be found within, why they see in natural identity a font of inclinations to be tamed rather than an objectivity to be respected, examined, and cultivated. I would ask furthermore: why should objectivity be a construction – beginning from a God, from a transcendental object – and not a respect for what exists? And also: why do they define and impose as objectivity what is a product of their auto-reflection, a necessity of their consciousness, and place it before the knowledge of existing reality?

In other words, I would contest their supposed objectivity with the argument that it is a product of their imagination. I would dispute the suggestion that using this given objectivity as a point of departure is a valid method for everyone and that it respects everyone's freedom.

I would ask them why what exists before or around them should appear as a dream when compared to their constructions.

It was this way in their era and it is the same today: what is fabricated or constructed is construed as reality while reality itself is confused with a dream.

Once this confusion occurs, freedom is not free: it does not return with sufficient radicality to its pre-given conditions, conditions which cannot be reduced to natural propensities placed in opposition to the becoming of the spirit. Indeed, what do the words "inclinations", "instincts" and the like mean? Of what are they the trace? Might they be the memory, the symptom of a relationship that is still uncultivated with the body, with the other? And why should their intention be evil?

Why does the blossoming of their nature not form part of their freedom?

Why do they lack a culture which spiritualizes the body, even though some cultures provide them with an example?

From where does their desire to represent everything as alienation arise? Why does being free require a distancing from the self? Why do they not elaborate a culture of sensibility or privilege a reawakening of the senses, of the perceptions, as the Far East does in its traditions?

Why should freedom force us to abstract ourselves from ourselves, from what we are before even dreaming it, before inventing its name?

Then I would ask them why they oppose passivity with activity at the level of sensibility. Why would it not be possible to be active and passive at the same time? Could my becoming not be an aroused passivity, an attentive activity, for example? Or even an affection that is both passive and active?

Such a perspective requires that we renounce the ideal of mastery and that we consider passivity in a way other than as a decay of the instincts, unless a transcendental object keeps us in suspense.

Above all, I would ask these philosophers if their need both for God and for the transcendental object to achieve their freedom is not derived from the erasure of the other as other.

The other as such, the other who guarantees irreducible alterity, belongs to the gender which is not mine.

The other of sexual difference remains inappropriable by me. I cannot reduce him to an object, to a possession, to a good, nor can I know him or appropriate him with the aid of my intellect. He always remains outside of me, as a thing in itself or a transcendental object.

But the object in this case is a subject. We are no longer dealing with a game between one person and himself, but with a relationship in which the other corresponds to a contiguity, to an empiria, to a simple factuality, to a simple ideality, to a pure and inaccessible transcendence.

The other of sexual difference is simultaneously contiguous to me and transcendent to me, subjectively and objectively: he is body and spirit, body and intention, inclination and freedom.

As such, I can long for him, desire him, but if he remains transcendent to me as other, my inclinations can neither be satisfied nor can they alienate my freedom. The other's transcendence leaves my sensibility both passive and active. It obliges me, moreover, to cultivate my inclinations to the degree that I desire the other or am attracted by him/her. In this way, desire becomes an opportunity for self-cultivation, and a cultivation of this sort always unfolds through a respect for intersubjectivity, in which my nature represents an objectivity and even a transcendence for the other of sexual difference.

One thing is true for me: becoming the woman which I am corresponds to an equally absolute ideal or objective which, for the philosophers that I have mentioned, is a becoming which is completely masculine and which has meant, in a certain sense, becoming God.

But becoming woman also means maintaining for man – and for other women – the framework of transcendental objectivity.

With the endless contiguity interrupted, a device is found which makes transcendence accessible.

Such transcendence does not lie in a beyond which is fabricated by me as a result of the necessities of my consciousness, or in an imposed beyond which alienates me.

Transcendence unveils itself in the other who is here present to me, but irreducible to my rational perception, if not as other.

The other of sexual difference returns me to my sensibility and to a necessary cultivation of it, while still respecting its tie with corporeality.

The other of sexual difference forces me to an elaboration, to a transformation of my inclinations, leading me to open my desire to a transcendental dimension in my relationship with the other as other. My freedom remains freedom only if the other remains transcendent to me, and if I respect his freedom.

From then on, freedom is founded in nature and in reason thanks to this relationship with the other.

We are very far away from claims issued against the other, very far away indeed from simple slogans, from propagandistic platitudes. To become free is, at this point, tantamount to a new duty which we must fulfil.

11

How can I touch you if you are not there?

The time dedicated to long-distance communication often leads to the loss of the sense of time itself, to a forgetting of the temporality which is necessary for our lives and for our exchanges with others.

There are different explanations for this. Among them are the following: 1) what we receive through telecommunications often amounts to information which has already been selected, concentrated, focused in time, and is alien to the unfolding of everyday time; 2) placing the accent upon information, the language of telecommunications does not favor communication with whoever is watching or listening: there is not, or only in an exceptional manner, a dialogue between the person who sends the message, the one who speaks and the person who receives it, the one who listens to it. The exchange between the two is interrupted.

To these two losses of the experience of life's time another can be added: an alchemy of the sensible which frequently implies a passage from the living to the fabricated-dead in one's encounter with the world and with others.

Such a statement will perhaps be surprising: what is more "alive" – one could object – than a stimulating television broadcast? It is not so simple ...

Certainly, I perceive the program on television with my eyes: I see it, I hear it. It is, without a doubt, conceived in order to excite my sensoriality.

But such stimulations or sensible awakenings are very peculiar, and we are not sufficiently attentive to them. Turning on our television sets, we imagine that we are opening a door or a window upon the world, and that in so doing we are entering into a relationship with others ... This truth, however, is extremely biased!

If I speak to you here and now in your presence, I see you – excuse me if I use words which are slightly technical – with binocular vision. I perceive you as a living body, a body-volume which moves: in the house, on the street, in the landscape, a body which I put into perspective with my own two eyes.

In order to see you, I give you the attention of my gaze, I give myself to you in perceiving you, as you allow or offer me the chance to look at you. We are two living beings with eyes that are both active and receptive, both concentrated and free to encounter each other.

If this were not the case, we would run the risk of coming to blows. Above all, the other would not be perceived as other. You would remain an image of my world, nothing more. I would direct an eye toward you in order to distinguish, identify and classify you. The dialogue between our eyes, this first tactile encounter between us, would be lost.

What happens in a television show? Your image, transformed by the script of the broadcast and by the artifice of technicians, is imposed upon me flatly and with an orthopedic volume. And before my eyes can adapt themselves, it besieges me, it stares at me, it fascinates me with its multicolored absence of volume. If my knowledge, in particular my technical knowledge, is called upon to evaluate your performances, including the aesthetic ones, my sensible awakening to you becomes drowsy, falls asleep. All that remain are collisions, fascinations, sensory manipulations, tears in the subtle weavings of a between-us. The constantly fluctuating relations between us are replaced by a game of powers, including sensible ones. You attempt to seduce me beginning from your reduction to a-slightly-colored-mobile-and-speaking-culturally-framed-image. Whether it works or not, we will no longer encounter each other as two. Under the lens of the technician and the lens of my eye, you have lost the touching imbalance of your body in motion. We stare fixedly at each other's absence like two cyclopes incapable of embracing with their gaze.

Your presence on television has taken you away from our embraces. What it has added – perhaps? – to the excitement of our senses, is stolen from the alchemy of the between-us. Much time will be necessary to return to it.

And what will we make of this hole in our memory? Of this change in the level of our relations? A bit more of the imaginary? Do we not run the risk of dissolving the tactile sensibility of our relationships?

We are present only through the gaze: staring with eyes wide open at the television show, blindly listening to the radio. I am touched by you through words spoken by an image or through sounds broadcast with varying degrees of exactitude: all of which interrupts the reciprocity between us.

The harmony between my eyes and ears which assures our corporeal encounter comes about in a confused way. Sometimes I hear you – but where are you? – sometimes I see you, but completely changed: luminous but without volume, without weight or materiality. I see you, but who or what have you become? And how do I touch you, how am I touched by you through such metamorphoses: in presence, in representation? How do I protect the memory of you, of us, despite so many changes in distance, in coordination between sound and image, despite so many scissions between the time to see you and listen to you, to see you, to listen to you and to place my hand upon you?

Where are you? Where are we? And what have we become?

I observe an apparition which I find to be more or less pleasing. I hear voices which are more or less familiar. But the proximity of your body at the intersection of our eyes and ears, in the reach of our hands, in the smell and taste of our bodies, this happiness in our encounters has disappeared in a multiplicity of images, in words where truth or a more or less mendacious seduction are concentrated, in an acceleration of time, in a multiplication of possibilities which take us away, bit by bit, from the eternity of a moving rediscovery of each other.

Between my fingers, you have become a phantasm, a star for everyone, a carbon copy, a fashionable representation, an ageless reproduction, an impalpable beauty, an evanescent flesh . . .

I know that you are still incarnate, that you still have a material consistency, that you occupy a space within the air: an obstacle which is always resistant to the various waves which we produce or which produce us, always resistant to the collision between two bodies. But how can we approach each other, dispersed as we are into different streams? Your image upon my screen is no longer synchronized with your voice, abducted by the radio or by the telephone. You are in the ears of another while I request your presence. Your most precious message is addressed, perhaps at this very moment to . . . – to whom? – through a fax. Your hands move with efficiency, but the taste of the palpable is dissolved into useful or fashionable gestures.

Today, contact means a telephone number, not touching each other through our senses, our skin. Hello? I call you. You have left your message. I hear your voice more or less distorted by the answering machine, a bit more metallic, higher, sharper and at the same time exhausted. You tell me that you are leaving the country in preparation for a broadcast on the intercultural prospects of the future Europe.

The program will be in English. Your compensation – not bad at that ... – will be paid in *deutschmarks*, a check in the black is not assured ... In any event, you will not come back tonight, but probably for the weekend. You seem a bit stressed. Let us hope that this difficult performance on the international and, perhaps at some point, communitarian stage will not cost you too much.

Your delayed words have left me like a zombie. A flight or what? There you are with an unforeseen professional advancement. You fly away. It is truly fantastic. Except for us.

I do not know when I will be able to see you again. Your face, your image are outside of my reach at this point, and we no longer speak the same language.

In case you ever need it, I send you a note which says: "How about a Sunday in the country, the place where we were last year at this time. I hope that it still exists ... Meet me at 10:00 at my house. I'll be waiting for you."

We will roll about in the grass, sleep in the sun, take a bath of silence. We will eat many blackberries. Sticky and completely stained, colored, slightly disguised, masked: neither too close nor too frightened to meet each other. Us, who? Our surroundings will help us to rediscover each other without being seized by panic, despite our metamorphoses.

Perhaps we will embrace each other with our eyes, unite our voices, barely brush against each other: picking blackberries, pirouetting on the grass. We will communicate in the smell of the fields, of the woods, in the damp and burning heat of the midday hours, in the taste of fruit. Perhaps we will not be two, not really two, but we will be alright, a bit relaxed, a bit closer. We will send each other several signals or signs of recognition, to be deciphered later, during our trips, for example. Unless we are dreaming. Who knows?

It is possible that a great deal of time will be necessary to

interpret these gestures of ours. When they are deciphered, will
we not be forever distanced from each other? We are too preoccupied with knowing what is taking place between us. We speak of
this or that thing, we know about it more or less, we still enquire
about it, and communicate in these mutual revelations. But to us
and about us, what do we say? Sometimes, exasperated by such
silence, one throws oneself upon the other to rob him of his secret.
Disappointed, we return to what has been communicated to us as
news of the day, of the week, of the month. Nothing has been
said about the truth of what we are. And this outburst has not left
me the time to taste your skin.

But, Sunday, weariness will spare us of such fruitless attempts.
We will be immersed in the happy and drowsy inertia of a lazy
afternoon. The air, the sun, the grass will touch us, will speak to
us: we will allow ourselves to languish in this work of nature. For
us, the week will be finished and we will do nothing.

In spite of everything, I have a great desire to be with you. But
how will we succeed in being present and together at the same
time? Here an entire history must be examined: not only yours
and mine, our small misunderstandings and differences, but also
that of a culture which for centuries, and still today, does not
allow us to be two, as two, with each other.

It all began with a culture imposing on us an ideal which is
unearthly and alien to our perceptions, to our corporeal senses.
Such an ideal separates us, as does an abstract model, in theory
valid for both of us but, in fact, impeding our coming into
presence with each other. For centuries, we have been zombies,
reduced to the condition of phantasms by means of what has been
proposed as truth, as good. Beauty is certainly less simple: but only
just, I would say. Who has taught us to perceive the whole within
the horizon of beauty? On the contrary, it has often been repeated
to us that we are not up to such a task.

And instead of looking at you, looking at me as body and
"soul", instead of contemplating and approaching each other as
bodies animated by an interiority, we have invented bodies which
are ideal, invisible, impalpable, different from those which we are
for each other, here and now. We have imagined each other to be
gods or devils, angels or demons, rather than man and woman

(men and women), present to each other in this world, in the sharing of our becoming. We have decided that what we touch with our hands is never as real, good, or beautiful as what we produce with our intellect.

We have made each other into images and sounds outside of our own sight and hearing. We have conjured up representations or doubles of ourselves more perfect than we are when present to each other. We have imagined reproductions of men and women which have exiled us from ourselves, prevented our coming together, removed us from the touching between us: with our eyes, our voice, our hands, our skin, our smells.

We have sought each other outside of ourselves, not as we are. We have distanced each other, while desiring to embrace. Looking up to the other as an ideal, we have supposed him to be where he cannot be found: in the abstraction of an idea, in the perfection of a model, in the distance of an idealization, in the flatness of an image, in the insensibility of a dead thing . . . We have not thought that the ideal could correspond to the mystery of an intention which inhabits the other, making him desirable. We have located the cause of enchantment beyond the other, outside of him, reducing him to an object of attraction, to a cause of sensations, to a seductive image, to a fascinating representation, without imagining him as a mystery to be examined, contemplated, embraced, and not sought in the beyond.

Little by little, we have lost the habit of looking at each other, of listening to each other, of touching each other, of perceiving each other. We have looked elsewhere, or we have remained in the night saying: I love you.

And have we not, at last, returned love to the beyond? Loving what we could not touch with our hands, see with our eyes, hear with our ears. Desiring what was outside the reach of our senses, without bothering to train our perceptions for desire: learning to look, to listen, to touch. The other here present has become an inanimate object, an artificial presence, a cause and an accomplice of decline: of loss of aspirations, ideals, energy. At most, we have made an *alter ego* of him.

But how do we caress an image? Is it not already cold, insensible, dead?

Have we not been disappointed by an approach in which we seek life, warmth, happiness? We have consoled ourselves by dazzling ourselves even more, organizing competitions for the most fascinating spectacle, for the most extravagant masquerade, for the most artificial appearances. We have remained pure nature: woman who gives birth, sexual tension which grows or subsides, causing changes in the body and in sentiments, etc. By becoming so many masks: we have lost our sight, and, above all, our sense of touch. With each one imprisoned in his or her own sphere or transformed into a single, fused matter, how could we ever caress each other – in such variable conditions? We have never found each other as two present to each other, two speaking to each other: with eyes, voice, hands, body . . .

Always separated or reduced to a single embrace or to a single deluge, always divided between one who is subject and one who is object, one who is active and one who is passive, one who has intention and one who remains nature and experiences it, we have not built a between-us, and such a lack has left us in the hands of the language of the television set.

Originally separated by an ideal, a model imposed from above, we find ourselves in the same position thanks to the many distances which have multiplied in number and in magnitude through the workings of a generalized techne. In our age of sexual liberation, we have lost the sense of touch – a strange paradox of a culture which unveils its foundations, its presuppositions, its underside, its secrets.

Lord, are you listening to me? I am not so sure . . . I shout towards you from underneath a flight path. Yet I have invested all of my savings (and a part of my father's) in finding peace in the forest: there is no gas, there is no sewer system, the trash is removed only once a week, the closest store is four kilometers away. Peace at last, I thought . . .

To be touched everywhere and all the time by her – who, according to you? To live according to her rhythm – mine apparently. To breathe, to look, to listen, to taste in a tactile way. To be bathed in the air and to caress her infinitely different works with tenderness. To remain for entire hours contemplating through all of my senses, through all of my skin.

To rediscover a bit of life, of happiness.

A true paradise . . .

*

You have considered this hermitage too beautiful for me. You have reminded me that the earth is only the earth. Which one? Do you find that airplanes are really useful? For what? To distance you from me, from yourself, at an extremely rapid pace? To lose the sense of gravity? To go more quickly without knowing where you are going? To fill up bank accounts only later to provoke crashes in the stock exchange? (You have to have fun, don't you?) To carry exotic fruit here, while farmers must throw away our own? To make us forget when the sun rises and the spring arrives (I have even been admonished, in a radio program, for not remembering this)? To poison the trees and disturb the flight of the birds? To multiply relationships without living any of them? And again, to what end? To convince me that this earth is a place of exile?

But such blackmail does not work. I love this earth. It fills me with its favors. My senses and spirits rejoice in it. It bestows everything upon me without weighing me down with anything. Its goods are in harmony with my everyday needs and desires. All that remains for me to do is to find a roof and a few clothes, but the rest comes from her: the fruits of the earth are sufficient to live.

I praise whoever respects their natural growth, whoever cultivates them and gathers them when the sun or the rain permit it. Some farmers, above all the women, offer them to me modestly, hardly daring to utter a price. Often, a gift is added to what has already been weighed and calculated. A chaste intimacy binds us together when these fruits of the earth (good, colorful, flavorful, with touching shapes and skins) are passed from their hands to mine. If the harvest is abundant, sharing is assured, with the exception of those things which require many hours to be cultivated and gathered. "How can I haggle over what the earth gives in abundance?", they apologize, adding fruit to my order: "It is the season, make the most of it!"

I celebrate the fecundity of the earth, singing the praises of her workers.

Lord, this place would be a paradise, were it not for the airplanes. I have already doubted you because of certain animals which carry fear or sickness with them. Airplanes and other machines which destroy the planet and us arouse suspicion in me as well. Your omnipotence seems to get confused with men's dreams of omnipotence. If you are truly a good and powerful Father, why do you allow your faithful believers to commit such foolishness?

But I do not think you hear me anymore because of the flight path. And if you were to respond to me, could I hear you?

As for the majority of your ministers, they talk and talk, even using the mass media. What do they discuss? According to them, useful things – among them, a fear of you. Do you realize this?

I have already lost some of my hearing as a result of the noise they call culture. If I listen to them, I risk losing even more of it.

Allow me to worship you, to revere her, by contemplating the flowers, listening to the birds, tasting the fruits of the earth. All of your favors are welcome if they add to the innocent happiness of life. And if they help us again to be two.

12

A mystery which illuminates

Never have I experienced the difficulty of addressing women and men together as I have in writing this book. How do I speak to you at the same time, my female and male readers? I know several of you, I dialogue with some of you, and I am not unaware of the joys and even the difficulties of our exchanges. I long for these exchanges because of what they reveal to me, their discoveries, but also their opacities or nights. I want them for their resources and the affective asceses which they bring with them. But this is the first time that I feel so intensely the difficulty of addressing myself to you, women and men, with the same words.

Nonetheless, I want to do it. But how do I realize my intention? It does not seem that the difficulty can be overcome: I do not wish to discuss the same realities or idealities with you; I cannot reawaken your hearing in the same way, or even attempt to do so. I find myself confronted with an insurmountable obstacle, before an upside down angle, yet wanting to return to an image. I am faced with an angle lacking a vertex which would allow two paths to converge, meet each other and unite, thus making communication with the two genders together possible. If a vertex of this sort exists, we are not aware of it, at least not yet. I must, therefore, assume the risk involved in addressing myself to you in the knowledge that I may not be understood by you, impossible as it is to communicate with women and men in the same way.

The desire to speak to you together, to you who are of different genders, collides with the experience of having nothing possible to say.

Historically, this nothing has been discovered by a discourse which is intended to be rational and neuter, rationally neuter. Such a language forgets that we are women and men, neutralizes this dimension at the level of meaning, and sends us back to the home, to the bedroom, in order to live it . This gesture denies the important role which belonging to a gender plays in defining subjectivity, rationality, truth.

I do not wish to reduplicate this cultural blindness. Instead, I want to elaborate a way of thinking which takes sexual difference into account, which refuses a transcendental reduction (Husserl) or a becoming of the spirit (Hegel), both of which consider us asexuate subjects.

If you are asexuate, I have nothing to say to you. In this case, my words would appear to me as unreal, mendacious, artificially abstract, devoid of ethics or truth. I could be very technically able, very erudite but, in my own eyes, my teaching would remain worthless.

I am, therefore, confronted with an aporia, to use a word from philosophy and theology, even if this aporia is of a new type. I find myself facing a difficulty which cannot be overcome by language.

What do I do?

There remains the possibility of pursuing a critique of a monosexuate discourse, which I will do. I could also attempt to expose, from time to time, the truths that are more appropriate to one gender or to the other, and I certainly will do this as well.

But the aporia remains intact.

Dwelling upon the question of the other might be a way to deal with it. But the problem of who the other is is not an easy one, supposing that one can still use the words other, others. I do, in fact, address others, but these others are so different that speaking simultaneously to both genders reveals an insurmountable aporia.

There remains nothing else to do but to approach this aporia and perhaps elaborate a phenomenology not only of what exists, what appears, but also of what does not exist and what cannot appear: a way of addressing myself at the same time to all of you, men and women.

I would like to remind you in a few words why placing discourse in the neuter is not a desirable solution: it presumes to reduce you to the neuter before knowing who you are. Who knows who or what woman is, who or what man is? To whom will I speak? In attempting to place discourse in the neuter, I would utter words not anchored in reality. I would expose truths which are only appearances, and not the appearance of truth. My speech would not have any meaning. Moreover, in order to overcome the aporia, I would use power: in the name of science, in the name of philosophy, I would return to the neuter, and such a garment would disguise the truth with a semblance and an appearance which would erase our boundaries. Instead of considering the truth of our differences, I would mask this truth with a lie which does them violence. Neither woman nor man, I would not achieve the minimal capacity required to convey any sort of truth: the capacity for chastity as woman. Sublimating my sensible immediacy seems to be a condition of my authority to speak of truth. I must recognize that I am a woman and, remaining such, I must also be able to differentiate myself from my immediate sensibility.

I must, likewise, turn to you, women and men, with a respect for your gender which is unsustainable in natural attraction – if I am not to risk making speech and hearing impossible between us.

The device for thinking and transmitting truth must be reinvented and given a new foundation in sexual difference. In the absence of such a foundation, the word remains a form of power which is unreal and deceptive, a means of seduction which forgets reality and respect for the other. It is of no use, therefore, for me to attempt to communicate with you, nor is it enough for you to try to listen to me: no true speech is possible.

The elemental condition of the word can and must be founded upon the recognition and the sublimation of our sexual, sexuate reality.

At first glance, it seems simple, but it is extremely difficult, because everything, or almost everything, must be reinvented.

But in our age, there are many things that need to be rethought! For example, we must restructure the relations between love and thought. The relationships between sensibility and thought, between affective life and the life of culture still remain unelaborated, at least within our tradition. And the same can be said about the cultural elaboration of our to be woman or to be man. We must devote ourselves to the same task: how do we speak, how do we speak to each other beginning from the reality which we are, beginning from the inclination and the love between us: woman and man, women and men? How do we communicate between us in our everyday lives, and also at the level of thought, at a philosophical level which can be taught, transmitted, without returning to the neuter in an artificial and violent way?

This task requires that we abandon the opposition between

nature and word, that we give up the idea that a true word can be foreign to our bodies, to love, that it can be neuter towards them, towards us.

Such a word may have been a bridge or a framework during a part of our history, but this does not imply that it must exist in a way other than as a framework: for waiting. The framework must not be confused with the truth. It only represents a means for approaching or unveiling the truth. Today, it often seems that we confuse the two and that what is called truth is merely the structure for sustaining it.

As regards the other, the error of a neuter word is clear: it is neither true nor ethical. However, I do not believe that the correct remedy is to oppose truth to ethicality. An analogous opposition appears between Emmanuel Lévinas' and Jacques Derrida's thoughts about the other.[1] For Lévinas, a philosophy of the other is above all an ethic; for Jacques Derrida, who bases his reasoning on the works of Husserl and Heidegger, the philosophical question of the other is not foreign to the question of truth, to the question of the to be.

From my point of view, it is not necessary to separate truth from ethicality, to separate, in other words, ethicality from the question of the other's to be. Since the other is – is already, perhaps will be, has been, has in himself a seed of the to be in so far as he exists – I must respect him as the other which he is.

This alliance between ethicality and truth would open a new age of thought, of philosophy: language, the constitution of the subject, cultural values would take care of bodies as elements of nature to be spiritualized and left as bodies, would preserve hearts as organs of life and of love which are irreducible to logical alienation and reduction, would sustain the measure and form of a reason which is capable of cultivating them in their truth, in their affects, in their differences. In short, they would take care of us as the women and men that we are, in body, in heart, in words.

At the beginning, there is an aporia. We lack the words for such a thought. That does not mean that it is impossible, or meaningless, that it represents an unfeasible utopia. We simply do not have it now.

Experiencing the lack of a word, an obligatory silence, is not easy. But denying it means refuting the experience of reality and truth. It also means not recognizing the other as an other who is different from me, foreign to me: neither me nor mine, nor *alter ego*, nor the same, nor like me.

Beyond its philosophical and ethical necessity, today the recognition of the other represents the possibility of a future for us in a variety of ways.

The age of science threatens us by means of an exteriority which never returns to us, by means of fragmentation, the alienation of the object of analysis, that is, in an objectivity which no longer corresponds to that of a subject or to a subjective consciousness capable of thinking for itself and developing its history.

Technology uses the language of the neuter: a disincarnate language, a universal language which pretends to be valid for everyone, beyond our differences. Such a language already speaks through machines more quickly and more correctly than we do, and this represents a challenge for our bodies, our hearts, our thought.

This danger exists, above all, as a result of the loss of a living and present relationship with the other. In the reign of the computer, the other is no longer: we are all equal, copies which are more or less alike, more or less capable of using this machine, of being used by it, at the cost of generation and of the rebalancing of meaning through our relations with others. We have become more or less unnecessary as human beings, separated through the formal language of computers which now force their law upon us without knowing who we are. The existence and becoming of our to be are subordinated to technological programs.

In order to resist their domination, it is necessary that we hold on firmly to our incarnation and to the real and present relations between us: woman and man, women and men.

If the risk posed by techne for man's future truly exists, this is probably so as result of two characteristics of our tradition:

1. Language – the *logos*, as it is called – has been considered a technical means for taming existing reality, for creating ideal models which would be preferable to reality itself. Such a tendency, which might for a time have been at the service of the constitution of the human subject and of his world, today turns against them. When techne appears as the reign of an abstract

ideal which commands us, it no longer serves us as the women and men that we are. It annihilates us in the neuter.

2. From the beginning, the relationship with the other has been considered as a genealogical one in our tradition. Such a reduction of the question of the other is probably tied to the privilege enjoyed by the patriarchal family as the model of social organization: both civil and religious.

We have considered the other as Father (or son) and as brother, while through necessity subjugating fraternity to paternity, the other of the everyday to the Other as father.

This model, which was constructive for a time, appears to be a source of non-truth, of non-ethics, in particular, but not exclusively, for the reality of sexual difference.

With this in mind, I will turn to the philosophy of Emmanuel Lévinas.

According to this philosopher, the face of the other appears to me through the face of God (the other resembles God, and I see the face of the other thanks to my relationship with God). Respect for the other, an ethical relationship with him is possible thanks to the passage through the absolute Other: God.

This method, this ethical way seems mistaken to me for many reasons, even if it is a mistake not always easily uncovered or avoided.

1. Respecting the other in the name of God means imposing *my* God upon him, not respecting him as other.

2. Lévinas' God is bound to a language, a language imposed upon nature – micro- and macrocosmic – which constitutes a people. This idea of a people does not consider the bodies, the hearts, the words of women and men to have equal value. For Lévinas the man, the passage through his God is, perhaps, an imposition of limits upon his instincts, upon his natural intemperance, but does not represent a way of respecting the other as other. Instead, it might lead to the other's subjection to an absolute of reason, of spirit, of the power of *one* discourse which, in the name of God, deprives him, and above all her, of a transcendence which is appropriate to him, to her.

3. Placing God between the other and me prevents the present dialogue between us. The Other includes us in the same discourse: we speak only in his horizon, in his truth, assuming that this is

even possible. In a certain sense, we no longer speak to each other: we update or repeat something which has already been said. The singular authority of a God as envisioned in the masculine does not favor communication between the two genders: man and woman.

4. The God of Lévinas is not incarnate, sensible, perceptible to the senses: he remains faceless. How does one see the face of the other through this invisibility? For Lévinas, perceiving the other, contemplating him, encountering him in the present, in presence, takes place thanks solely to a morality already composed of language, a morality alien to real incarnation, here and now. Certainly, I will respect the other to the extent that I cannot kill him, rape him, etc., but not as body and language which are present to me in their becoming. The other is always already placed in a moral context, defined by written words, which distance him from me: the other is already in the past, a past in which laws and customs are more suited to the masculine than to the feminine subject.

In order to respect the other, I must leave simple morality behind. I must think of him as a body, as a heart, and also as a present word. I must consider him a singular incarnation which resists already existing language: I must hold on firmly to him as to a singular sensibility, thought, and truth. Behaving towards him in an ethical manner, in the name of my values, is the same as destroying him in his alterity. In reducing the other to a moral dimension of my life, I have already isolated myself from his alterity, his truth, and also from a possible Other.

The other is two. Would not subjecting him to a single language, to a single truth, involve destroying him as other? Certainly, passing through a God in order to respect the other does not appear to be the best way of recognizing either gender. When doing this, I can neither love the other in a sensible way nor leave him his life. He finds himself within the horizon of my law: I obey my law instead of recognizing the other as other.

This way of proceeding will not guide me further in my becoming, will not help me to walk between love and thought, or escape the abstraction and violence of the neuter. (Lévinas condemns this in the philosophy of Heidegger, but he himself does not seem to escape the neutralization of the other or the danger which comes from science and techne.)

In order to approach the other while respecting and safeguarding his alterity, perhaps we can take as our point of departure the following corporeal, affective and intellectual reality: the other is a mystery.

Recognizing that the other is and will remain a mystery for me, I can:

respect him as other without subjecting him to any of my laws;

marry ethicality and truth in my relationship with the other: I think of the other as the mystery which he is for me, as a truth, certainly, but always as one which is unknown to and inappropriable by me, unable to be dominated or universalized;

change the relation between love and truth: respecting the mystery of the other through love implies that this respect for a truth which will never be mine modifies my, our relationship with the truth.

Instead of being light opposed to darkness, or knowledge opposed to ignorance, truth is light which does not give up mystery, light which illuminates without revealing; never total, never authoritarian or dogmatic, but light always shared between two subjects irreducible to one another.

This respect for the mystery of the other represents a positive and negative path towards him, or her. In so far as I am confronted with such a mystery, it represents the same towards me.

If our culture were to receive within itself the mystery of the other as an unavoidable and insurmountable reality, there would open up a new age of thought, with a changed economy of truth and ethics.

Beyond transforming our relationship with truth, the mystery of the other would allow us to enter into a philosophy, and not only an ethics, of love, into a thinking of subjectivity as inter-subjectivity.

The mystery of the other, the irreducibility of a mystery between us, makes possible:

– the renunciation of the opposition between adult and child, father and son, an opposition which has subjugated the relationship with the other to genealogy;

— the horizontal definition of the relation with the other as other: not the other who is necessary to me as father, nor the other, often necessary to him, as son (see for example Lévinas' discourse on alterity), but the other who is tied to naturality;

— a horizontal thinking of the relationship with the other which through natural and spiritual necessity – ontical and ontological is found in a philosophy of sexual difference.

If the mystery of the other were reduced to the observation that his and my history are not the same, we would not actually be dealing with a mystery: it would be a secret which could often be recounted, explained, and named. This so-called mystery is presented as an empirical given which reason can attempt to explain, reveal, and interpret.

The other, whose mystery will never be a shared secret, the other who will always remain a mystery to me, is the other of sexual difference.

Only by considering this mystery as irreducible can we begin the construction of intersubjectivity: physical, sensible, thinking with the other as other.

Such an elaboration (a philosophical one, in particular) is based upon the recognition of a mystery which will never be revealed: an idea which has remained foreign to Western thought up until now.

Sketching this new horizon in philosophy, founded upon an inappropriable truth, involves, as a first gesture, a necessary respect for the virginity of the other. It is a prerequisite for establishing a philosophy of sexual difference and of intersubjectivity.

If this were to come about, virginity would not be reduced to a natural reality, would not be ascribed only to the feminine or to the neuter, but would be the other name for the fidelity of each gender to itself, with a respect for the other gender.

Virginity is, in fact, the necessary condition for the existence of a word which is present here and now between us: woman and man, women and men.

Virginity is the other face of an aporia inhabiting a word which heeds sexual difference. The absence of a like discourse suitable for the two genders, the need for an almost absolute silence between them so that they might begin truly to speak to each other: these things which are impossible to say must be said in order to respect the virginity of each person as a proper identity conscious of its limit.

13

Epilogue

To Return to Her

Where has the time gone? Where have I vanished? Days have
passed without gathering, nights without stars. I have lost the path
of light and am left without forms to protect the duration. Does
duty remain? But fidelity to the to be has faded away.

It seems, at times, that there is no longer anyone and that the
world's relationship with itself has dissolved, that people no longer
speak the same language. Only the birds still turn themselves to
us. And the stars, perhaps?

A crack in the obscurity of the sky, a glimmer in the unknown
of the crowd, a word, a smile – a sign, an invitation.

To return to her, to rediscover the spring. Eyes open upon the
light. Attentive to the moment, the body tastes the air anew,
innocent of every care, of every obligation, if not those of perceiving, praising, immersing itself in her, and being reborn.

The happiness of rediscovering her rises – familiar, noisy. Still
more populated with birds, trembling with living presences. As in
a feast offered to our perceptions, to our attentive senses. And the
friend, up there, faithful.

I slip into her, the only one so in existence – warm and fragrant,
beautiful to see, flowering and virginal, silent and rustling. I await
what will be born of me in word and sound capable of singing
her humble perfection.

Will I thus be healed of every injury? If not, I will remain in
the artifice of an energy foreign to me, to her.

The air: wonder. And you of so many colors, which few
consider. Between themselves, humans rarely speak of flowers.
Noisy and busy, they go along their own path. How can they
remain with those who are voiceless?

And as for me, why should I sing if silence is sacred? If praise lives outside of the word? Certainly, singing is fidelity, but it interrupts the to be together. And where is the highest faithfulness?

Sometimes desire wants only silence. Before or after the sun, it is pleasant to rest in the penumbra, in a still light. In the palpable intimacy of the air is the invisible which frees the gaze, awake without looking. Trust is made vigilant, attentive to what occurs in simple self-abandonment.

The sky is grace. An almost sonorous light is diffused, immobile. The summer gives itself like a tranquil and complete happiness. Harmony of the senses is its splendor.

To emerge to another life. To perceive it through the whole of me. To savor it, and thus to find strength, serenity. To reach the end of lacerations and abandonments. To sense life, its tones, its fragrances – true communion.

I allow the taste of experiencing to exist. I rediscover sensibility, escaping judgment, exiting prisons. I breathe nature, I impregnate myself with her. I become her, I become me, stronger, more faithful, capable of staying, of protecting. Of growing?

To love together with her, porous to a multiple familiarity. Is it a self-gathering more profound than the one which takes place in the silence of life and in the presence of so many guests?

But with you and without you, is this the same? Is the perception of her changed today? Is happiness other? More peaceful and more intense? A quiet[a] beatitude in which the universe and you are joined.

Loving her, to love you. To discover and to preserve you, through her, thanks to her. Colors and harsh sound have become an intimate touch. There is the consolation of returning to myself unharmed by a lack, whole and ready for you. Perhaps freely tied to you.

I have been distant from you, I have not spoken to you, I have not listened to you for a long time. And there are many noises which separate us. If we were to speak to each other, would there not again be a silence? If we were to listen to each other, would the sky not become cloudy? If you were to return to me, to you, would rest not follow: aroused tranquility, attentive joy?

A bit of your presence and I rediscover myself within me – life. Contemplation occurs, as does touch, being touched, grace. Desire and love return. You are here and there is no one: only the whole.

Only a second and joy blossoms. Restored strengths, soothed wounds, joy flows from the growth of intention. Mixed within it are elegance and decision, righteousness and flexibility, the sweetness and loftiness of thought.

I seek to maintain myself with rigor and agility, light in necessity, free from the suffering which results from incompleteness.

I intuit my path, I perceive the quality of our future encounters. There is only a touch of happiness, evidence in the pain of doubt. There is nothing. But maybe it is enough to foretell the way, in order to rise a bit. Would not the tenor of the air be the best omen for me?

Beyond the common atmosphere, I am attracted by what allows me to reach a new age. Thus, I flee from a faded environment, from a tepid swamp, from an undifferentiated weaving, towards a birth which is still in the future. And, just perhaps, towards the arrival at you.

I want happiness for you, for her. With steadfastness, I try to keep myself on the path of joy. I sense myself in the air, finding peace again. Around me and between us, there is a space. I am immersed in life. I intuit height as happiness itself. I experience the breath as elevation. I rejoice in light, in wind, in spatiality. I await the impossible, listening to the stars.

I savor what already is, and what is often forgotten in the present.

To perceive altitude in this way erases, purifies. Another place is opened, a nest located on high, a lofty but humble abode. It holds a reserve of air, an almost palpable secret. Sometimes a chaste and strong wind arrives, capable of brushing, of approaching, of playing with presence. It brings comfort and compels being.

To return in me. To close my lips, gathered. To cultivate the breath as a prayer and to prevent the dispersal of this animated cloud, this living mystery. To condense them as the substance of joy, and not to allow them to sparkle or to shine, to take shape or name. To preserve only what maintains attention in itself, nothing more: in order to remain faithful to oneself, to the other, in happiness.

I walk from such freshness towards you. I remain on the summits, yet I love to you – sun in the mist, heart in thought, judgement suspended, contemplation foreign to the object.

The closed lips guard memory, sealed upon a mystery which no word will tell. Does a form make it present?

Each of our days should shape a form, or each of our encounters should give birth to an alliance between two rings. It is not something which we must exchange, but perhaps a dwelling, a place to remain, a circle to inhabit, a limit in which to rest.

The air here is fresh, white in a certain sense. The quality of the air and its voice are related in a tonality which lifts the soul, removing it from the abysses, from the ambiguities which still enslave it.

Between his words and the cosmic universe, a harmony invites her to an alliance which does not require it to renounce itself. It enters into a new cycle as into an invisible glory. It will never again be what it was, but its becoming unfolds without death or resurrection. A general transubstantiation is at work. All of nature is changed.

Air,
you the pure,
you who make confusion vanish,

you who render each to him or herself, the exterior to the
    exterior, the interior to the interior,
you who flow between one and the other but without destroy-
    ing either's boundaries proper,
you who respect the skin and nourish it, and who procure the
    medium for every contact,
you who maintain life, protecting it beyond every morsel gaudy,
you without whom we cannot touch each other,
who always keep yourself between us, whose distance allows us
    to approach each other,

you who distinguish each from the other and assure that each
    never resembles the other, except through actions which
    want to be alike but not in growth as such,
Air,
you who protect us from fire and ice,
who allow us a heaviness not simply subjected to gravity,
you who leave to sounds their tonalities.
Air,
if you are missing, which presence will look after us?
And how do we make you, if we are made by you?
Certainly, there are words.
But, when uttered, do they preserve the breath?
Is there a breath in them which can bring about a future
    existence?

And how do we pass from nature to spirit without you? And
how do we give soul to the body, for the first time and always
anew, leaving it to be body if you are lacking? Is it not thanks to
breathing, to the breath, that such a task can be carried out?

And also, thanks to love for the earth, to the love between us:
to the desire for you, air, who circulate from her to me, and who
move from a more physical to a more relational or mental part in
me. Without air, how would the passage from corporeal attraction
to affection, to the word take place?

And how could we share both corporeal inclination and spiritual
taste or touch, if the air did not make itself the vehicle for passing
from one attraction to the other?

If I remain matter while you impose yourself as word, the air
loses its meaning for my becoming and for our exchanges. It
remains a means of survival and does not accede to the role of
mediator for its own growth and for cohabitation.[b]

The spiritual life rests upon the imposition of figures which are
already represented, of words which are already codified. They
rob us of being present both to the world and to each other
through the air – free, inhabited, breathed, spoken. Whatever the
truth that they convey may be, they steal from us the element
which nourishes life: the body, love, thought.

And how do we heed their message before training the breath?
Where will it be inscribed in us, where will it enter us if we do
not open a place of breath to welcome it: to receive it from outside

and from within? Without blind submission or rejection, time begins to put truth to the test of life, to the test of the union between fire and wind, between the heart and the breath.

And thus in order to encounter the world. And thus in order to encounter you. If my desire wants only love, as the earth wants only the sun, I lose the path of becoming: for me, for us. I fall asleep in a tepid or burning atmosphere. I am no longer capable of cooling the air because of its elevation to the word, to sharing. Far from rousing a bit of wind for our exchanges, I suffocate the breath in fire and there remains nothing but cinders.

At best, I will discover myself in the sea. From there I can be reborn, it is true. But I fear losing the way to me, to you. I fear having to restart everything from the beginning again and again. And thus to infinity.

In the air which is invisible everywhere, but nonetheless there: to touch you, to be touched by you, as in a game.

The wind blows between us. I try to seize it, but the breath separates us. And, the more I long for you, the more the air escapes me.

I breathe the air which has inspired me. I praise it and rediscover my way: freedom, height. This place is mine, perhaps ours. Each of us leads the other to it. If each cultivates the breath, perhaps we can meet – to savor the air together, to love life in her. To play in order to be and to become simply alive, in body and in soul.

To protect both you and me, to remain two, I must learn love. I must descend into the heart, keep the breath there, not exhaust it in work, not paralyze it in the mind. I must harmonize it between the shoulders. Until wings grow? Folded around me, they help me to remain in myself, to keep me from leaving myself for any reason, to resist seduction, violence.

I contemplate the outside and the inside. I think without renouncing you, me, us. I love to you, I love in me. The breath comes and goes – life, affection, intention. In me. In two.

Author's Notes

I   THE WEDDING BETWEEN THE BODY AND LANGUAGE

1   Regarding this, see *I Love to You: Sketch of a Possible Felicity in History*, (trans. by Alison Martin) Routledge, New York and London, 1996; *Sexes and Genealogies*, (trans. by Gillian Gill) Columbia University Press, New York, 1993.

2   See *Being and Nothingness*, (trans. by Hazel Barnes) Philosophical Library, New York, 1956.

3   J.-P. Sartre, op. cit., p. 394. This chapter refers, as does the following one, to the section of the book entitled 'Concrete Relations with Others'.

4   Maurice Merleau-Ponty, *Phenomenology of Perception*, (trans. by Colin Smith with revisions by Forrest Williams) Routledge and Kegan Paul Ltd., England, 1962, pp. 166–167.

5   Ibid, pp. 169–171.

6   Emmanuel Lévinas, *Totality and Infinity*, (trans. by Alphonso Lingis) Dusquene University Press, Pennsylvania, 1969, pp. 257–259.

3   DAUGHTER AND WOMAN

1   *Being and Nothingness*, (trans. by Hazel Barnes) Philosophical Library, New York, 1956, pp. 423–424.

8   BETWEEN, US, A FABRICATED WORLD

1   This is the translation cited in Martin Heidegger, *An Introduction to Metaphysics*, (trans. by Ralph Manheim) Yale University Press, New Haven, 1959, pp. 146–148.

2   Ibid, pp. 157–158.

12 A MYSTERY WHICH ILLUMINATES

1 See Jacques Derrida, 'Violence and Metaphysics: An Essay on the Thought of Emmanuel Lévinas' in *Writing and Difference*, (trans. by Alan Bass) University of Chicago Press, Chicago, 1978.

Translators' Notes

I PROLOGUE

^a There is a play on the two verbs *raccogliere* and *accogliere* throughout the text which is difficult to render in English. *Raccogliere* has a variety of meanings which include "to collect", "to harvest" and, figuratively, "to gather one's thoughts" or "to meditate". *Accogliere* means "to receive" or "to welcome", and we have made use of both of these options depending upon the context. We have translated *raccogliere* as "to gather", "to collect" and, on rare occasions (especially when it is in the reflexive form), as "to meditate".

^b The word used in the original text is *senso* ("sense") which allows L. Irigaray to make use of the ambiguities and different meanings therein.

^c *L'universo* ("the universe") is a masculine noun. Thus, when L. Irigaray uses the pronoun "him" (in Italian *lui*), she is both making reference to and personifying the universe.

^d The pronoun "her" *(lei)* refers back to the feminine noun "earth" *(la terra)* and accomplishes the same process of personification that we noted above.

^e We have, according to L. Irigaray's wishes, translated *l'essere* as "the to be" in an effort to remain faithful to the title and project of this work – *To Be Two*. This gesture is more in accord with L. Irigaray's repeated use of verbs in the infinitive to establish their link with the infinite.

^f Readers of both the Italian and English texts should note the editorial error in the Italian version. Clearly a question, it is placed in the form of a declarative statement in the original text.

^g L. Irigaray has informed us that the original text is in error here. The Italian version reads "... *acconsento in canti di lode.*" It has been modified to "... *acconsento con canti di lode.*"

2 THE WEDDING BETWEEN THE BODY AND LANGUAGE

a Readers of the English translation of *Being and Nothingness* should note the shift from the gendering of the "other" as masculine in Sartre's original text to the gendering of "other" as feminine in the English translation of the chapter "Concrete Relations With Others". Barnes' explanatory footnote on page 390 (*Being and Nothingness*, Philosophical Library, New York, 1956) is instructive: "The pronouns in French are masculine because they refer to *autrui* ('the other') which may stand for either man or woman but which, grammatically, is masculine. The feminine sounds more natural in English."

b It it worth noting that the Italian word *cultura* can mean both "cultivation" and "culture".

c *Enti* and *esseri*, respectively. The entire sentence in question is: *"Siamo due tessuti da corpi e parole, enti ed esseri, e non soltanto enti stregati da un padrone o che svaniscono in una sognata verginitá."* While traditionally *ente* has been translated as "existent" and *essere* as "being", we have, again at the encouragement of L. Irigaray, translated *ente* as "being" and *essere* as "the to be" (or simply "to be") in order to highlight her innovative use of these concepts. They will reappear throughout the course of the text.

3 DAUGHTER AND WOMAN

a In the following paragraph, L. Irigaray will gender all of the active adjectives as masculine and all of the passive adjectives as feminine.

b *"une transcendance quelconque"* or *"una trascendenza qualsiasi"* – Note: We have referred to the original text (*L'être et le néant*, Éditions Gallimard, Paris, 1943, pp. 475–76), as well as to the Italian translation used in the original version of the present volume (*L'essere e il nulla*, [trans. Giuseppe del Bo] Il Saggiatore, Milano, 1965) in order to highlight concepts important for L. Irigaray's subsequent analysis of this passage.

c *"une transcendance quelconque"* or *"una trascendenza qualsiasi"*

d *"une transcendance quelconque"* or *"trascendenza qualsiasi"*

e *"une transcendance vivante et indifférenciée"* or *"una trascendenza vivante e indifferenziata"*

^f *"une transcendance quelconque"* or *"trascendenza qualsiasi"*

^g *"cette transcendance indifférenciée"* or *"questa trascendenza indifferenziata"*

^h *"une même transcendance indifférenciée"* or *"una medesima trascendenza indifferenziata"*

4 TO PERCEIVE THE INVISIBLE IN YOU

^a This word appears in its English form in the Italian text.

^b L. Irigaray has noted a mistake in the original Italian text. In place of *godimento*, which would be translated *jouissance*, she has inserted the word *provare*, which we have rendered as "experience".

^c L. Irigaray has found another flaw in the Italian original: *". . . il desiderio d'amare"* (". . . the desire to love") has been put in place of *". . . il desiderio d'amore"* ("love's desire").

5 I ANNOUNCE TO YOU THAT WE ARE DIFFERENT

^a L. Irigaray has determined that the Italian text is in error here: *". . . il desiderio in due"* should replace *". . . il desiderio a due"*.

^b "Him" *(lui)* – a reference to the sun *(il sole)*, which is a masculine noun.

7 TO CONCEIVE SILENCE

^a L. Irigaray has changed *". . . si può realizzare"* (". . . can be realized") to *". . . si può riscoprire"* (". . . can be rediscovered").

^b This is a reference to Hegel's *Begriff*, which is variously translated in English as "notion" or "concept".

8 BETWEEN US, A FABRICATED WORLD

^{a-b} In the original version of this text, L. Irigaray makes use of the Italian translation of Heidegger's text (*Introduzione alla metafisica*, Mursia, Milano, 1968) in which "strange" is translated as *inquietante* in both instances. However, in Heidegger's German text, the words used are *Unheimliche* and *Unheimlicheres*, respectively (*Einführung in Die Metaphysik*, Vittorio Klostermann, Frankfurt am Mein, 1983, p. 155). The very basis of

Heidegger's analysis in this section of "The Limitation of Being" is the translation of *deinotaton* as *Unheimliche* and readers are referred to his full discussion on pages 148–206 of the English translation. We have translated L. Irigaray's subsequent use of *inquietante* here as "uncanny" and not "strange" while noting the reference to the above passage.

ᶜ See page 157 of *An Introduction to Metaphysics*, where the quotation is translated as "...breaks out and breaks up, usbricht und umbricht, departs and plows, he who captures and subjugates".

ᵈ See also pages 166–167 of the German edition previously cited.

ᵉ L. Irigaray has found an editorial error in this sentence as it appears in the Italian. We have translated it according to her changes. The original sentence reads: *"Così a poco a poco ha creato un mondo che si interpone fra lui stesso e un mondo al femminile."* It should read: *"Così a poco a poco ha creato un mondo che si interpone fra lui e se stesso, fra lui e un mondo al femminile."*

9 SHE BEFORE THE "KING"

ᵃ Here, *esso* and *Esso*. We have used a dual meaning to convey both the impersonality and the actual gendering of this construction.

ᵇ⁻ᶜ The opposition in the Italian text is between *primo ministro* and *prima ministra*. The translators are here presented with a particular difficulty for the simple reason that English does not gender nouns. Although the English word "legislator" is much more vague and might convey a less lofty political title than "prime minister", it is one of the few English words whose Latin root *(legum lator)* is clearly masculine.

ᵈ *"una qualunque trascendenza"*

ᵉ *"L'amore era il legislatore..."* The masculine form "legislator" is here used because it refers back to and describes the masculine subject "love" *(amore)*.

10 EACH TRANSCENDENT TO THE OTHER

ᵃ A significant change has been made by L. Irigaray to the Italian text. The original reads: *"Ho fatto l'esempio di Dio come esteriorità che non può alienare la mia libertà perché questi filosofi hanno bisogno di Dio, mentre desidererebbero non essere accecati, alienati, resi non coscienti, non liberi.*" It has been modified to read: *Ho fatto l'esempio di Dio come esteriorità che non può alienare la mia libertà perché questi filosofi hanno bisogno di Dio, mentre desidererebbero non esse*ne *accecati, alienati, resi non coscienti, non liberi.*"

b   "*un trascendentale qualunque*"

c   "*una qualsiasi opera dell'uomo*"

d   "*una qualsiasi creazione di un Dio*"

13 EPILOGUE

a   L. Irigaray has made another noteworthy departure from the original text. The Italian version is written in the following manner: "*Beatitudine, quiete nella quale l'universo e te si congiungono.*" This has been changed to: "*Beatitudine, quieta nella quale l'universo e te si congiungono.*" The change involves *quiete,* which has been changed from a noun to an adjective *(quieta)* modifying the feminine noun *beatitudine.*

b   L. Irigaray has changed *condivisione* ("sharing") to *convivenza* ("cohabitation").

Index of Names